Liberty and Justice for Her?

Liberty and Justice for Her?

A New Paradigm for Ambitious Women

CONNIE WHARTON

Wharton Publishing
Lubbock, TX

© 2012 Connie Wharton

All rights reserved. No part of this publication may be reproduced, stored in retrieval system, or transmitted in any form or by any means electronic, mechanical, photocopying, recording or otherwise, without the prior written permission of the publisher.

Published by
Wharton Publishing
Lubbock, Texas
www.ConnieWhartonLeadership.com

Publisher's Cataloging-in-Publication Data
Wharton, Connie.

    Liberty and justice for her? : a new paradigm for ambitious women / Connie Wharton. – Lubbock, TX : Wharton Pub., 2012.

    p. ; cm.

    ISBN13: 978-0-9852870-0-9

    1. Wharton, Connie. 2. Women executives—United States—Biography. 3. Businesswomen—United States—Biography. 4. Success in business—United States. I. Title.

    HD6054.4.U6 W43 2012
    658.409082—dc23   2012901956

FIRST EDITION

Project coordination by Jenkins Group, Inc.
www.BookPublishing.com

Interior design by Brooke Camfield

Printed in the United States of America
16 15 14 13 12 • 5 4 3 2 1

Dedication

To my husband, I love you more every day

To my smart and independent daughters, who every day affirm the promise of talent and ambition in women

To my mother, whose unconditional love and uncompromising optimism will always be the beacon in my life

In loving memory of my father, who instilled confidence and ambition in a young girl, and who was my greatest champion

CONTENTS

ACKNOWLEDGMENTS ix

I WONDER... xi

INTRODUCTION
A Personal Note to My Readers xiii

CHAPTER 1
The Connie Wharton Story 1

CHAPTER 2
Why the Lack of Improvements? 25

CHAPTER 3
The Burden of Isolation 55

CHAPTER 4
Taking Control of Your Home and Your Career 75

CHAPTER 5
Durable Relationships and Networks—and How to Build and Use Them 99

CHAPTER 6
It's Different at the Top 125

CHAPTER 7
The Responsibility and Accountability of Men 145

CHAPTER 8
Executive Women in Their Own Words   157

CONCLUSION
Independence Day   187

APPENDIX 1
Leadership Programs for Women   199

APPENDIX 2
Further Reading   203

About Connie Wharton   207

ACKNOWLEDGMENTS

A special thanks to Margaret Z. Couch

In the early stages of this book's development, my dear friend Margaret Couch was a co-author. Her insights, feedback, and suggestions are evident throughout this work. She shares a passion that all women be the best that they can be, and that they be fairly recognized and equally rewarded. Her recent publication *Women Who Listen to Horses* is a beautiful and inspiring work that feeds the soul and calms the heart. Her friendship, advice, support, and sense of humor are among my most valued life treasures.

WITH GRATITUDE TO:

Ed Myers   A ghostwriter extraordinaire. His infinite patience, good humor, and wonderful writing skills made this journey a joy. Most importantly, he allowed me time to absorb, to think, and to learn as the book progressed. I know we both believe that the book is a better work because we allowed the research and facts to drive deeper insights and understanding.

Chuck Nielson and Jill Campbell   The two people most responsible for whatever success I have had. Both were in my life at the right time and the right place. If only every woman could have the benefit of the wisdom and teachings of these two . . . .

Iris Newalu As the Director of Smith College Executive Education for Women, Iris provided knowledge, insight, and encouragement. She and Smith College provide incredible leadership programs for executive women. And as their program for men gains traction, it may well become the leading catalyst for change.

Interviewees To the women portrayed in Chapter 8, thank you for your honesty, your willingness to share very personal revelations, and your insightful experience regarding ambitious women. When I found myself losing steam, I thought of all of you and pushed onward.

Background Interviewees To all the men and women who gave of your time and experiences in the early development of the book, thank you. It was your universal confirmation that equality is still an elusive element at the top of U.S. corporations that provided the urgency to see this project through.

To WICT, the Betsy Magness Leadership Institute, and my Betsy fellows Thank you one and all. This wonderful organization and all the programs and support they provide to women in cable and telecommunications are unparalleled in any other industry. They are a shining example for the world to follow.

To Jenkins Group, Inc. For helping people like me.

I WONDER . . .

... Why fewer than 4% of Fortune 1000 CEOs are women?

... Who is responsible for the failure of U.S. women to have equal representation and reward in Fortune 1000 companies?

... What is the role of current CEOs, both individually and collectively, to address this shortfall?

... What current female board members and female executive officers are doing to effect immediate, sustainable, and significant improvements in this arena?

... What women need to know and do to insure that their ambitions are fully recognized and equally rewarded?

... If men think there is inequity at the top echelons of the Fortune 1000—and what they think should be done in response?

... Where the indignation is among women who haven't attained liberty and justice in our corporations?

... Why women are still reluctant to speak their minds on this subject?

INTRODUCTION

A PERSONAL NOTE to MY READERS

As a child, I was constantly encouraged and told that I could be anything I wanted to be when I grew up.

Throughout my adult life, I looked the other way or dismissed my personal feelings about women and independence and equity. I believed in "Liberty and Justice for all"—for all men and all women. I was raised to believe that hard work, honesty, and integrity were the only requirements for fulfilling one's ambitions.

During my twenties, life was simple: keep your head down, work hard, be a good wife, and you will live happily ever after. That's exactly what I did throughout my twenties. I put my husband through law school, landed an entry-level job with the largest employer in Texas, and I worked *hard*. I was deemed a "comer" in the corporate world—and I was off and running.

It all blew up in my thirties. I gave birth to two children in quick succession. My husband and I both had highly successful careers, and those careers began to compete with each other. As the only woman professional and manager in my company during those early years, I constantly tried to fit in as best I could. However, I began to suspect that all wasn't as I had been led to believe. "Liberty and Justice for all" seemed to mean different things to men and women. I felt totally alone. So I worked harder both at home and in my professional life. I pretended that everything was great. But a nagging question was always in the back of my mind: "Where were all the ambitious and successful women?" Companies were spending millions of dollars—first on affirmative action plans, then on diversity and inclusion. What was wrong? Why didn't anyone notice?

In my early forties, I checked out. Convinced that I couldn't be both a good mother and a great leader, I made the wrenching decision to leave the company I loved. Three and a half years later, once I felt rested and my children were a little older, I began my second career in the cable industry. It was during this phase of my career that I discovered my own power and independence. I met other successful women and achieved personal and financial goals I'd never thought possible. While this phase of my life and career was significantly better than the early years, there were still unanswered questions about the likelihood of ambitious women being recognized and rewarded in numbers similar to our male peers.

Why are women still so underrepresented at the highest levels of our corporations? What is holding women back? The nagging questions were getting louder—and it seems that as a country, we have stalled. The "pipelines" are full of talented women, but something is still blocking ambitious women from getting to the top.

I've researched and written this book over the last two years. It represents my own personal quest for the underlying reasons of gender inequity. It is a search for the truth. In the beginning, a friend and I interviewed many women and some men in hopes of finding

A New Paradigm for Ambitious Women

differing opinions and perhaps a few answers. What we found was a legion of women and men who believe or acknowledge what is contained in this book. It was something of a shock—and certainly a disappointment—to find many otherwise smart, ambitious women who conceded, "This is just the way it is."

My hope is that if we can better articulate the truths about why ambitious women are not achieving reward and recognition comparable to our male peers, then we can really begin to effect fundamental, sustainable change. Our country is in crisis. The American family unit has changed, whether we want to admit it or not. As women, we must recognize the need for independence throughout our lives. Crisis always presents opportunity.

The opportunity now at hand is for women to reach out and grasp the recognition and reward for fully realized ambition. It is okay to be a full partner in your marriage. It is okay to expect your employer to demonstrate how they will achieve gender equity. It is okay to expect actions and results in a reasonable time.

This book is for all the men and women who truly believe in equality and are willing to look at hard truths. Where there is truth, there can be transformation. I still believe in liberty and justice for all.

CHAPTER 1

THE CONNIE WHARTON STORY

My toes curled over the edge of the starting block at the end of the pool. The sky was blue, the day was hot, and the smell of chlorine in the air was strong. Parents and spectators screamed and yelled. I felt both terrified and excited as I looked out across the pool. My entire body tingled with excitement—and as the starter's gun went off, I shot off the block. I was only six years old, but I already knew how much I wanted to win.

What transforms a small-town girl into a corporate executive? For me, the journey came about through a combination of hard work, strong will, excellent mentoring and parenting, and a little luck. I didn't know it at the time, but I would also benefit greatly as corporate America began to open its doors to women in senior leadership and executive roles.

I want to start by telling you my story—not to focus on my experiences for their own sake, but because those experiences raise interesting questions that affect all women in leadership today.

Then I want to talk about defining moments of my career and my reflections about the entire experience.

I was born in Charlottesville, Virginia, but my family moved a couple of times after that, so I spent most of my years up until my sophomore year of high school living in Ottumwa, Iowa, a town of about 30,000 people. My dad was a psychiatrist; my mom was trained as a nurse, and she alternated between working as a homemaker and working in my dad's office. My dad was quite forward-thinking for the times, and my mother certainly wanted abundant opportunities for her only daughter, so my parents raised me and my three brothers (I was the oldest kid) pretty much the same. As a team they were equals in my eyes. Dad may have been The Doctor, but Mom was The Rock. I didn't feel that they treated me any differently just because I was a girl. All four of us kids swam competitively, and my parents encouraged me just as much as they encouraged my brothers. I had a wonderful childhood, and I explored many interests—sports, ballet, and playing violin, harp, and piano. But most importantly, my parents also instilled strong values, discipline, and a determined work ethic in me: during high school, for instance, I worked as a lifeguard, and I continued working other jobs during college. More than anything else, my parents raised me to be tough, independent, and accountable for my actions. I grew up with the promise that if I worked hard enough, I could be anything I wanted to be.

I have to admit that my college career was nothing to boast about. I didn't feel especially inspired or energized by my undergraduate education; however, I loved the experience of being away from home and being on my own. My aspiration was to become a professional dancer, and I'd had good training for many years. However, I realized at a summer camp sponsored by the New York City Ballet Company that I was good but not great . . . and that I was never going to be a prima ballerina. Although I considered the option of becoming a dance teacher, I majored in psychology at Southern Methodist University in Dallas and graduated in 1973. I didn't have a clear game plan at that time. I married my high school sweetheart, and I went to work to put him through law school. Then I found a second love: my work. Although college didn't inspire me or seem to capture my imagination, the corporate world fascinated me from the beginning. And, after all, I had been raised by parents who told me that I could be anything I wanted to be. What could possibly get in my way?

MY CAREERS—AND WHAT THEY REVEAL ABOUT WOMEN IN CORPORATE AMERICA

I've had three wonderful careers and many excellent mentors, and I feel very fortunate to have benefited in countless ways from my workplace experiences. It wasn't really until after I'd left the corporate world that certain issues started to nag at me more intensely than before. This is definitely one of those situations where backing off provides some perspective. In addition, I finally had time to consider the issues more closely. In this new and unfamiliar situation, I didn't feel concerned about what anyone might think about what I said, and I didn't have a company or boss whose expectations I had to meet. I've started to evaluate what I've learned over the years—as well as what I've heard from other women—and to explore where we stand at this moment, as well as where we need to go in the future. I have finally had time to really think and ponder.

Women have advanced a lot in recent decades. We now have routine access to many opportunities that we never had before. I believe that over the past eight or ten years, however, change has slowed and maybe even stalled. We've come a long way since the passage of the Civil Rights Act of 1964; at the same time, I believe that some of our biggest challenges still lie before us.

According to "Pipeline's Broken Promise," a report published by the Catalyst organization, less than 4% of CEOs in Fortune 1000 companies are women. One level down from that, only 15.6% of all executives are female. In addition, pay for women in those positions lags behind pay for men, especially at the CEO level. More bad news? Unfortunately, it gets worse: these statistics appear to be stagnant. The typical senior management team of eight to ten people in many corporations will generally have at most one female member. You would think that by now, women would have much better representation in the executive suite, but we don't. Far from it.

This situation isn't acceptable. Men *and* women in corporate America must openly acknowledge the gap, and we need to do more than say, "We're making progress." Where are the goals, the accountabilities, the timetables, and the consequences for falling short? If we believe that men and women have equal intellect, and if many barriers to women's advancement have diminished, what explains the breakdown at the top? In my first career, I was often the only woman at the table—or even in the room. When I left Texas Instruments in 1993, there were still only three or four women vice-presidents. Some years later, in my second career, when I interacted more often with other executive women, we would often look at each other and ask, "What's going on here? Why are there still so few of us?" And now, as I look back and look ahead, I can't help but ask, "What will it take to move the dial? If the outcome isn't where it ought to be, what are we going to do about it?" I also have to ask this question: What are women really missing? Well, for starters, we are missing power, influence, and money. We are missing *equality. We are missing the promise of equal opportunity.*

I don't believe that people in most corporate settings decide with malicious intent to suppress women. Instead, the outcome is just a result of how the system works—a result of how it's been forever. Men built corporate structures *for men* and *for men's benefit,* and these structures are still generally headed *by men.* While men may not be individually *responsible,* they certainly should be held *accountable* for the state of their respective corporations. Even if there's no malice aforethought and no willful gender bias, these outcomes are still unacceptable. Women should be better represented at the upper rungs of the corporate ladder by now. And unless we take definitive action, the situation isn't likely to improve any time soon.

This book offers both an exploration of where women stand in the corporate hierarchy and how individual women—this means you!—can advance our careers. Before we delve into these issues in depth, however, I want to describe my careers and "where I'm coming from." I'm starting our discussions in this way not to toot my own horn—though I'm proud of my careers—but to explain what I've experienced and how these experiences have shaped what I believe must happen to advance the interests of all women in corporate America. Many of you will see yourselves in my shoes. I hope you do, because my struggle is probably very much like your own struggle. My hope is that the book will echo many of the things you have thought or observed over the years.

Texas Instruments—"I'll Be One of the Guys"

After graduating from college, I was living in Lubbock, Texas, with my husband. He had just started law school, so I took the very first job I could find, which just happened to be as a contract security guard for Pinkerton Security. Yes, armed with a fresh college degree, I'm pretty sure that I started at the *very bottom* of the career ladder. Once I signed on, Pinkerton placed me at the brand-new Texas Instruments facility that was opening up in Lubbock. I sat at the front desk where, as the receptionist, I greeted guests, checked their credentials, and kept an eye on who entered and left the building. I worked for Pinkerton for three months; one thing led to another; and soon TI hired me to be an entry-level human resources professional. I was off and running, even though I wasn't quite sure where! It's worth noting that the primary reason my boss (who later became my mentor) hired me was that I'd spent a summer during college backpacking with a group of guys across Europe. He thought that demonstrated initiative and a little daring. Not many women were doing that in the early 70's. Why was this significant? Well, I was already being selected because of traits that many people would consider more characteristic of men.

During my first seven years at Texas Instruments, my husband and I didn't have children. Even then, I intuitively felt the need to get my career going before starting a family. Truth be told, I was fearful about how in the world I would handle both. I worked constantly for my first seven years—60 to 70 hour workweeks, just like all the guys. And I loved it. I worked nearly every Saturday. Although Saturdays were "casual," you were still expected to be present. It wasn't that the company wouldn't cut you any slack for personal or family issues, but who would have asked for it? I recall that when I was pregnant with my first daughter at the age of 29, I asked my boss if he thought my having a child would be a problem. Would it be acceptable, for instance, if I didn't come in on Saturdays? His answer was disconcerting: "We'll have to see." I didn't get any reassurance or acknowledgment of the yet-to-be-articulated notion of "balance." That attitude was just a sign of the times. Fortunately, the timing of my early parenting years coincided with some changes. Texas Instruments was just beginning to understand the impact of long hours on productivity and employee morale, so the company made a policy that limited the professional workweek to 45 hours. Better yet, TI paid entry-level exempt employees overtime, so they eventually dropped some hours as a cost-cutting measure. Soon, the "just showing up" Saturday workday fell away altogether.

TI was a very macho environment, as was generally true of the entire technical business sector. It was and remains a highly competitive company. Everybody was tough. We were primarily a defense contractor and a manufacturer of semiconductor components, so the employees were mostly engineers and manufacturing people. While many women worked on the assembly lines, men held most of the higher-paid technical and management jobs. To be a female executive and a mother was an unusual combination in those days. I gave birth to two children in sixteen months, and I went back to work the first time just eight weeks after delivering and the second time after only six weeks. Even when I was at home, I tried to continue doing some work. I still remember one day when I was nursing a baby and working on a presentation at the same time. I also remember how alone that felt. There was no one to turn to with questions about how to manage home and work. That level of commitment and quick turnaround was really what the company expected. In this very male environment, I was intent on surviving—and on excelling.

Ironically, one of the great things my boss and mentor told me was, "Connie, you're going to stick out here like a sore thumb. If I were you, I'd figure out how to make that work." I knew I was different. I also knew that because I was different, I needed to fit in if I was ever to be trusted. Being different was *not* a good thing at that time.

It would be many years before anyone celebrated diversity—or, frankly, even accepted it. Something else: I knew not to rock the boat about anything personal. I didn't blush when there was massive cursing in the conference room, some of it of a sexual nature. This was back in the days of smoking, so I learned to smoke—that's just what you did. I'm tall—5' 7"—but I always wore three-inch heels, so that put me at about 5'10." I'd been an athlete in college, so I made sure I was viewed not only as a strong contributor, but as a physically strong woman. I never put any pictures of my family on my desk. Why? Because I was trying to fit in. Walking into my office, no one would have known if it belonged to a man or a woman. I would out-guy the guys. All of these approaches surely worked to my advantage back in that era. But I didn't realize I was also sacrificing my independence. I didn't realize I was working desperately hard to hide the fact I was a woman.

I excelled almost from the start. I moved quickly from individual contributor to manager to a director supporting a 4,500-person facility and worldwide offices. When I'd been working at TI for 13 or 14 years, I started getting offers for officer-level positions. I was young for that—still in my mid-thirties. My husband is a lawyer, and he'd been doing quite well. He didn't want to leave his law practice in Lubbock, so I turned down several offers from TI. (More about that later.) Finally, one offer came along when I'd been with the company about 15 years. The message that came with it: "Connie, you've said *No* a lot. This is a great offer—probably the best one you're going to get. If you say no this time, you may not get asked again." That wasn't said in a negative way; it was just—"Hey, either step up or step off." So I took the job.

That decision started what would be six straight years of commuting, either for me or for my husband. I moved to Austin for two years to take that first officer-level job. My husband, bless his heart, commuted to Austin for that whole time. Then, at the end of that period, TI went through a restructuring process, and the company wanted me to move to Dallas. I figured at that point that it might be a move to Dallas one year, then somewhere else the next. So I said, "Okay, but I'll take the job only if I can continue to commute from Lubbock." TI graciously agreed—and paid—for me to fly 325 miles back and forth between Lubbock and Dallas every single day. I got up at 4:45 every morning. I was in my office in Dallas at 8:20. I flew home on either the 4:30 p.m. flight or the 6:00 p.m. flight. That wasn't so bad—I had an hour of quiet in the morning on the plane and then another when coming home. I just learned to make it work, and I commuted like that for nearly four years. But eventually that situation ground me down physically, and I realized that it wouldn't get any better. I was also torn by not being able to give 100% to both my family and my work. I had spread myself so thin that I just couldn't make it work any longer. So, after 20 years at TI, I left the company, which absolutely broke my heart. I still love Texas Instruments, and I keep in touch with a lot of folks there. A little later on, I'll talk about my mentor at TI—an incredible man who drove me to succeed.

Cox Communications— "It's Time to Be the Lead Dog"

After leaving TI, I didn't return to corporate work for about three and a half years. I was a soccer mom, and I loved it. But when my kids got into junior high, I got restless again, and I knew it was time for me to go back to work. At the age of 47, I started looking around. I made the decision that if I intended to do something different, I'd make it a hundred and eighty degrees different. Eventually I took a job with Cox Communications—part of the Cox Enterprises Corporation, headquartered in Atlanta—and for about six months, I worked for Cox in Lubbock in a human resources position. This job at Cox paid about half what I had been making at TI. Why did I take this step "downward"? Well, that's a good question. My answer to myself—and to all aspiring women out there—is this: Sometimes you have to move backwards to find a new path.

Here's how it worked for me.

Two important events took place. First, my boss—our vice-president and general manager—left his position very suddenly. Second (and simultaneously with the first event), Cox acquired a very large cable system in our part of the country. The company asked me to become the vice-president and general manager of this operating unit during the merger under way at the time. It's important for me to note I didn't apply until I was asked. At this point I still didn't have any idea what I might be capable of achieving. Perhaps naively, I agreed to this offer. The long and the short of it was that I ended up being selected to fill that position. Our revenue was in the neighborhood of $300 million annually with 800 employees in 15 cities—a huge West Texas area that was large by any cable system standards.

The next year just about killed me. I didn't know the business, and, to be honest, I didn't know nearly enough about running *any* business. It was absolutely a trial by fire. I almost got fired, but I managed to pull the situation together in time and learn enough about what we needed to be doing. I was successful because I was a strong leader and because I knew a lot about organizational excellence. I also knew how to hire great people. In truth, my team got me through. About four months into this job, however—just when I finally thought I'd figured it out, and when I thought we were on a path to recovery—I discovered that a lot of really bad assumptions from the merger were built into our business plan. I was working for a woman named Jill Campbell—the first really strong female leader I had ever known personally—and she came to Lubbock to assess the situation. When I met her, I thought, "Interesting—a female boss! This might be even better than I thought." But during the course of our meeting, she said, "Connie, you and I seem to really get along well, and I like your style. I like a lot of things about you. But the numbers in your division are just crap. So—I'm giving you ninety days to turn it around. If you can't, I'll have to fire you." Then she got up and *hugged* me.

I was in shock. I'd never failed at anything in my life. I had always been the golden girl. While I wasn't totally responsible for bad assumptions in my business plan, I was totally accountable for turning the business around. Somewhere in that moment I found my strength and my passion. The fear of failure fell away and I became a true leader—and I knew I was destined to become a successful executive. It was much the same feeling I'd had when I was six years old and looking out across that pool in my first competition. I was going to win. Perhaps my sense of independence was returning?

So I dismissed my finance guy and replaced him with someone who, thankfully, knew what he was doing. Right off this new man discovered that we were $7,000,000 worse off than I'd thought. So we put together a plan for a turnaround. This was the most defining moment ever in my professional life. My team and I decided to put it all on the line. We were either going to be successful or go down giving it our best. One way or the other, though, I was going to be absolutely sure we did the best we could possibly do. In that moment, I became fearless. I wasn't afraid of failing. I understood that there's no dishonor in doing the very best you can do. I was afraid only of not having enough time. So we took risks—big ones. We worked desperately hard. In the end, we made it happen.

We *did* turn it around. Our division became a great success. I kept my job, and Jill remains a good friend to this day. We now laugh about those days. I was in that job for about six years. That was where I really learned how to be *the leader*. Before that, I was very much playing a support role. And I saw that no matter how successful I'd been during earlier phases of my career, I'd missed a lot of chances. It wasn't because anyone put me down. It's just that I was isolated—I had no women colleagues. It never occurred to me to question some of the things that I should have been questioning. I simply had no peer group. I had only one mentor, and although he was great, I was never independent enough to break away or explore other paths. Truth be told, I clung to him. I believed he was the key to my success.

But by 2005 I was successful, confident, and very happy. Then Cox decided to sell off all of the firm's geographically dispersed systems—20% of the company. My division was one of those to be sold. This situation led to the single best learning experience I ever had. But it was also one of the most intense and difficult challenges I have ever faced. I went to New York and Atlanta and presented to KKR, Lehman Brothers, Citigroup, and about 20 other venture groups and cable companies. The various Cox divisions were being auctioned off. While many people might be devastated by this development, I had learned to be fearless and strong, and I eventually recognized this situation for the opportunity it turned out to be. It was one of the most difficult and rewarding times in my life. It's also worth noting that I was able to work with another female VP/General Manager during this process. While we competed on one level, I believe we were great support for one another on a deeper level. She and I remain friends.

One other event truly changed my life at Cox—an event just as important, or perhaps even more important, than my specific job as my new career started. The first time I went to a Cox management meeting, I thought I'd ended up in the wrong place. I walked into this huge auditorium in a swanky hotel, and of the four hundred people there, half of those present were women and minorities. I'm looking around thinking, "Well, this can't be the company's senior management—there are so many women! Did the managers all bring their assistants?" But in fact the majority, if not all of their senior HR people, were women, and many were of minority backgrounds. A good number of the vice presidents and general managers, too, were women. I was just astounded. It was like the shift early in the *Wizard of Oz*—going from black-and-white to color.

In this way, Cox was a real wake-up call for me. After nearly 20 years in an almost all-male environment at Texas instrument, I started to see how different the corporate world could be. What had I missed? And *why?*

Time Warner—"Learning to Swim Fast"

After the auction of divisions at Cox Communications, I left Suddenlink, the company that had bought my division, and I went to a job at Time Warner that ended up being twice the size of my job at Cox. I was able to land such a lucrative job because of the networking opportunities I had developed when I was President of the Texas Cable and Telecommunications between 2003 and 2004 during my time at Cox. I benefited greatly from my relationships with TWC executives because of my work with the cable association. During my tenure at Time Warner, I ran a business that generated roughly $550 million in revenue annually. It was the largest Time-Warner cable system in Texas. I had a great time. Time-Warner is a tough company, but I had learned to swim fast, and I enjoyed my time there.

Aside from successfully running an extremely complex organization very well, I brought a Strong Woman initiative to Texas Time Warner. I gave much-needed funding to the Texas Chapter of the Women in Cable and Telecommunications. Today, that organization hosts an annual gala that recognizes great women throughout the state and raises their visibility throughout the entire industry. I mentored several strong women in my organization and developed enduring relationships with them. I offered support and encouragement to many younger women. Most importantly, I championed two women in a manner that required some risk on my part. I know that I will forever be a part of the lives of those two women. Later on in the book, we will discuss some action points to help women advance. As any good leader knows: if what you want to do is important enough, you'll find a way to make it happen.

In some ways, I miss the intensity of running a company. Stepping back from that role, however, has allowed me to get some perspective. To be honest, I don't like what I see happening to women in the corporate world. And I've reached insights that I believe are worthwhile for me to share.

As I look back on my tenure at Time Warner Communications, I have two reflections I'd like to share up front. The first is that when I started to work for TWC, I was the only woman executive at my level in Texas. When I left, there were four women in upper management at TWC. So, there's good news and bad news. The good news is that the numbers grew significantly. The bad news is that we didn't really help one another woman-to-woman. In fact, I believe we were significantly *less* supportive of one another than the men were of one another. This is a profoundly unfortunate situation! As women, we have to learn that we can have multiple networks and loyalties. We need one another.

This observation leads to my other reflection. In our current economic downturn, companies are consolidating and downsizing. I believe women at the executive level—not necessarily the CEOs but the executives who are one or two levels down—are most at risk. This point is one of the key premises in my book. The numbers of executive women has been stagnant over recent years. If, in fact, we are more at risk than our male peers in this economic crisis, we've reached a critical turning point.

DEFINING MOMENTS

A defining moment is a moment of realization, insight, and clarity. For me, these moments sometimes come from remembering an event that stood out at the time—but that may have occurred when I was too busy to evaluate the situation fully. Sometimes a defining moment means understanding an event that caught my attention at the time but made sense only later. Sometimes it means re-evaluating an incident or condition in a new light. All of the defining moments I'll describe concern women in the corporate hierarchy. In any case, I want to describe some of these defining moments now—issues that the rest of this book will explore in detail.

Defining Moment #1: The Boys Make the Rules

In 1973, when I got my first job at Texas Instruments, I was ecstatic. I was just 22 years old, and suddenly I was making twice as much money as most of my friends. I thought I'd struck gold! There really were no expectations about women at that time—only that you were damn lucky just to get hired. The expectations of me were the same as expectations of the guys. I had no inkling then that the workplace was designed by men—*for* men. I just wanted acceptance and recognition for work well done. In the years that followed, I had a very successful career. By the age of 34, I was the HR director of a facility with more than 4,000 employees. At 37, I became a vice president—only the second female vice president at the largest employer in Texas at the time. I was happy in that position and proud of what I was doing.

It was when I became an officer that I reached a crucial insight: no matter how good the situation might be, I was playing a game—*and the rules of the game were the boys' rules.* I had learned to play that game for my first fourteen years, and I played it really well. But the rules of the game are still the rules of the game. So, number one, you need to know the rules and understand them. Two, you need to make a personal decision about what's important to you—what your goals are, how you're going to reach them. The good news is that nowadays, there's much more awareness of this issue and how it affects women. There's more acceptance of women partly because there are more women present overall, since the sheer numbers make for greater balance. But the models are still much more oriented toward men, especially at the higher levels.

Defining Moment #2:
You'll Never Truly Be "One of the Guys"

At Texas Instruments—as is true in many other companies—leaders are often described as "strong," "aggressive," and "powerful"—words that are traditionally more associated with men than with women. There's no reason, of course, that female executives can't (or shouldn't) show these characteristics. In playing by the boy's rules, I suppose I tried to manifest these attributes in traditionally male ways to fit in with my male peer group. But whether doing so was a good idea or not . . . Well, that situation has been clarified in my mind over the years. Women can't be men. Women *shouldn't try to be* like men. As women, we have our own ways of communicating, of making decisions, of managing. Ultimately, trying to be something that's against our nature and identity can't fully work for us—and we can't win if we take this approach. Authenticity is one of the critical character requirements for a successful executive. It may well also be one of the most difficult attributes for a woman to demonstrate and exhibit in a male-centric world.

Defining Moment #3: You Need to Take a Hard Look at Your Work Culture

We all know that each corporation has its own culture. From the standpoint of executive women, I didn't completely understand what this issue could mean until I got to Cox communications. I'd been at Cox for only three weeks when I went to their first management conference. I mentioned earlier that I walked into the auditorium and found that of the 400 people in the room, half of those present were women and minorities. I did a double take: "Oh, I thought this was a management conference." And it was. But at Cox, management included women. The difference was just night and day compared to the electronics industry. The implications? Among others, it means that if Cox can be more inclusive and supportive of women, why can't other companies?

Defining Moment #4: Diversity Only Goes So Far

I headed up the first diversity program at Texas Instruments, so I'm aware of the issues inside and out. There's no question that diversity efforts have helped to foster the careers of women and minorities to some degree. However, these programs aren't truly advancing executive women's agendas at this time. When women start work after college nowadays, their pay is more nearly equal to men's in many fields—science, engineering, business, and so forth. It's later that the disparities grow. Why? We are just beginning to understand the "why" now. I'm not saying that the business world should abandon the quest for diversity. What I *am* saying is that on the middle and especially the upper rungs of the executive ladder, it's going to take far more than diversity programs to advance women's careers.

Defining Moment #5: "Hard" Stereotyping—or "Soft"?

To what degree are men in the corporate sector consciously, willfully holding women back from advancement? I'm sure this does happen at times—and of course it's a problem whenever it happens. Some men are certainly trying to hang on to the most powerful and lucrative positions. From what I've seen, however, I'd say that "hard" discrimination isn't common anymore. Instead, the bigger and more frequent problem is casting women in roles that are traditionally in a "support" capacity. This is an old story. And this informal set of assumptions, rather than overt sexual discrimination, is what I believe most often holds back minorities and women. There's been a tendency to perceive female executives as better at roles where communication and teaming are more important. The "soft" side of the corporation—HR, customer relations, and so forth—while the guys did the "hard" side—engineering, finance, and marketing. But the hard side was where all the decisions were made, and where all the higher paying positions tended to be. By contrast, women have been seen as better off in support roles. Yes, there are the Carly Fiorinas and Meg Whitmans of the world—but these women remain exceptions. How can we counteract the damaging aspects of "soft stereotyping"? I'll have a lot more to say on this subject later in the book.

Defining Moment #6: Childbearing and Parenting Are Still a Great Divide

I view childbearing and parenting as one of the "great divides" between men and women in the corporate workplace. It's true that nowadays, many men are more involved in parenting tasks than in the past. Unfortunately, the changes only go so far. Many male executives still don't see the situation with much clarity. The problem is that most companies won't accommodate women as they try to balance work life and home life. Also, men still tend to have much more linear careers than women, and male executives see their straight-and-narrow career paths as "the norm." This situation can lead to a frustrating kind of bias. As one male executives said to me, "I don't even like to hire young women until they're in their 30s, because before that, they haven't figured out if they want to be mothers or CEOs." As if we can't be both! Until we can somehow cross the divide that this statement reflects, female executives will face major obstacles to career advancement.

There's a critical time between the ages of 25 and 35 that is generally when women have their children. This situation is essentially what leads to a less linear career path for women than what men have. So what happens when you leave the workplace and then come back after taking time off to have your kids and to focus on raising them? It's hard to be taken seriously. One of the strongest beliefs in the corporate world is that by signing on to work at a company, you're making a nearly exclusive commitment—that you'll be there primarily for the firm. Taking time off means that you'll miss important events and will never catch up. Well, how crazy is that? But that belief is embedded—and it's still at the heart of the system.

Defining Moment #7:
Women Need Female Mentors

When I was at Texas Instruments, I didn't have many female peers. Toward the end of my time there, I knew a few women engineers, but that was it. I was the second female VP in the company, and by the time I left, I had only two female peers in total—and we did not communicate much at all with each other. One woman was far away from where I worked in the facility. She was an engineering manager, and I had great respect for her, but our paths never crossed. Since I was a senior HR executive, at that time it was politically risky for me to "reach down" to female managers at lower levels of the hierarchy. I had access to information concerning performance and pay, and HR people were sometimes reluctant to have personal relationships with others outside our function.

Later, during my time at Cox, there were a lot more women present; things were very different in that company. There were strong women present, and they were openly supportive of other women as women. If the guys didn't like it—they never said so! One of the first questions I asked a female fellow-executive at Cox was, "What would you do if the guys wanted to get together on their own terms?" My colleague looked at me as if I were an idiot and said, "Connie, they already do that—they always have. Haven't you ever been to a golf course?" Why did I have to be in my late 40s before I figured that out?

Defining Moment #8:
Women Need Their Own Networks

One of the most powerful experiences I've ever had throughout my executive career happened courtesy of the Betsy Magness Leadership Institute. This organization, sponsored by a trade group called

A New Paradigm for Ambitious Women

Women in Cable and Telecommunications, is designed to elevate women leaders in the cable and telecommunications industry. Over a period of twenty-five years, more than 400 women have completed this nationally recognized program to foster learning and to help them make the transition from being effective managers to becoming strong leaders. By creating connections within their classes, Betsy Magness fellows emerge with a committed passion to share what they've learned within their teams, their companies, and the industry as a whole. I was able to take part in this institute's programs ten years ago, and I can attest to its career and life-changing benefits.

The Betsy Magness Leadership Institute is designed for women in the telecommunications industry. However, my life-changing experience there prompted an intense defining moment: women everywhere in the business world need networks. Every female executive needs to find a network or build a network. Here's an important qualification, however: to be fully effective, some networks must exist in non-business settings. They can't be created by or "owned" by the company; that will lead to too many conflicts of interest. The company can nurture it, but the network itself has to be independent.

After my participation in the Betsy Magness program, I found myself looking back and thinking, "Well, thank God I finally discovered this." But I was 49 or 50 when I attended, and I was the oldest person present. The younger ones were in their mid-to late thirties, but they were still the up-and-comers. Better that I discovered it on the late side, however, than not at all! I believe what I'm describing is the single most powerful hope for women as we tried to change the numbers. As we examine the issues throughout this book, I'll have lots more to say about networks and enduring relationships.

"NOW—NOT TOMORROW, NEXT WEEK, OR NEXT YEAR"

As I said earlier, I've wanted to start this book by telling my own story because I believe these experiences have something to say about what other women face in the corporate world today. I also stated that my primary concern is what will it take to boost women into the executive levels of corporations in numbers and pay that are equal to men's.

Here's the big picture:

Women have made great strides in the workplace over the last forty years. More women are present in more different sectors and careers; women will soon be 50% of the overall workforce (and more than 50% in some sectors); and more opportunities are available to women than ever before. However, many crucial issues remain unresolved: ongoing disparity in pay levels; the limited number of women in high places; barriers to women's advancement; lack of corporate support for family issues that limit women's options; and others. No matter how much progress women have made, there's a long way to go—not just in the general workplace but also in the upper levels of the corporate hierarchy.

Thousands of qualified, experienced, imaginative female executives are fully capable of advancing into upper management and contributing their insights, abilities, and energy to the betterment of corporate America and to the service of corporations' clients and customers. It's a terrible waste for these women not to advance up the corporate ladder to the highest rung they aspire to reach. As the authors state in a recent article published by Catalyst (an advocacy organization for women): "Now—not tomorrow, next week, or next year—is the time for renewed efforts to uncover and combat systemic gender inequity."

A New Paradigm for Ambitious Women

I totally agree. It's now time to move beyond generalities about the factors that hold women back from the C Suite. It's time to identify the sources of this problem in specific terms—and then solve it.

CHAPTER 2

WHY THE LACK OF IMPROVEMENTS?

I believe you'll agree with me that the statistics I've presented in Chapter 1 make a clear case for change in the C Suite. Women are grossly underrepresented in top management. Given the great abundance of accomplished women in the middle ranks of corporate America, the dearth of female executives at higher levels can't possibly be the result of a talent shortage. Thousands of women nationwide are surely able and ready to move into the highest executive positions. Yet, as we've discussed, the numbers are stagnant. They may even be declining.

Why?

And, perhaps even more important: *What are we going to do about this situation?*

Before I offer my suggestions for change, I feel it's crucial for us to explore the causes of the current status quo. I'd like to do so by exploring several possible explanations for women's lack of advancement into higher executive levels. Central to this exploration are two fundamental issues: nature and nurture—biology and culture. Are women disadvantaged even before they set foot in the workplace? After we speculate about these issues, I want to examine how these two issues collide in the day-to-day reality of women's corporate careers.

SETTING THE STAGE: BIOLOGY

There's no question that some biological factors raise intriguing issues about the disparity between women's and men's levels of success in the corporate world. But do these issues *explain* the disparity? That's certainly the jackpot question—one I'll ask in various ways as we explore the topic. A pair of interesting factors are first, testosterone; and second, neuroanatomy and neurophysiology.

The Impact of Testosterone

Testosterone is the hormone notorious for stoking the fires of adolescent boys' wildness, contributing to some young men's juvenile delinquency, juicing up many men's aggressiveness, and fueling the male population's legendary lustiness. To some degree, these and other aspects of testosterone's reputation have a basis in scientific data. Testosterone unquestionably plays a huge role in males' development and behavior. It may even partially explain men's actions and behaviors—both positive and negative—in the corporate world. But the real situation is far more complex than it seems.

In most people's minds, testosterone is strictly a male hormone. It is indeed central to boys' and men's development—a factor we will discuss in more detail later in this chapter. Testosterone drives many physiological processes that make an embryo into a male baby. It promotes the growth of the male reproductive tract during fetal development; it influences boys' growth even before adolescence; and, during puberty, it fosters the dramatic changes that turn a boy into a man. Its powerful physical effects continue throughout male adulthood.

However, it's important to realize that women's bodies as well as men's produce testosterone. The female body produces about one twentieth to one tenth the amount of this hormone compared to what the male body does, but testosterone is nonetheless crucial for women to maintain the strength of their muscles and bones. In addition, testosterone is the primary sex-drive hormone for both men and women. Dr. Susan Rako, a Boston-area psychologist, states that testosterone is as much a woman's sex hormone as it is a man's. "The amount of testosterone . . . that a woman's body is continually producing," she writes, "is essential." Rako's book, *The Hormone of Desire*, eloquently describes the importance of androgens like testosterone to women's health.

Where does this situation leave us? And, more specifically to our discussion, can the difference between male and female testosterone levels help to explain the gap between the numbers of men and the numbers of women in the executive suite? This may sound like a reductive question, but it's worth asking. For many years—decades, actually—testosterone has been associated with aggressive behavior, competitiveness, and other attributes often regarded as characteristically male. Whether or not *specific* testosterone levels actually correlate with such behaviors isn't altogether clear. I learned several years ago, for instance, that some male litigators in some parts of the country list their "T levels" on their C.V.'s when applying for jobs. The tacit assumption here is that the higher the T level, the more aggressive the lawyer. A further assumption is that an aggressive lawyer is necessarily a good one. Well, maybe so. But has anyone done research to correlate lawyers' T scores with their actual track records in winning cases? I doubt it. Until recently, there hasn't really been much clinical research available suggesting how testosterone affects career choices or actions during a particular person's career.

In August of 2009, however, a story about recent empirical research appeared in both the technical and the popular press. *Forbes* magazine reported this story as follows: "Women with higher levels of testosterone are more likely to take financial risks than those with lower levels of the hormone, according to a study conducted jointly by the University of Chicago and Northwestern's Kellogg School of Business and published in the journal *Proceedings of the National Academy of Sciences*." This research had implications both for men and for women. In their experimental study, the researchers measured the salivary testosterone levels of over 500 male and female M.B.A. students, then compared the test results to the students' decisions regarding financial risk-aversion. This experiment involved assessing risk by means of a computer game. Participants had to choose either guaranteed sums of money (ranging from $50 to $120) or else a lottery with a 50-50 chance of winning $200 or nothing. The test results ranked participants according to the point at which they switched from the lottery to the guaranteed payment.

What were the outcomes? In women, the experiment showed a sliding scale of risky behavior directly correlated to testosterone levels: the higher the participants' hormone level, the riskier their behavior. Follow-up interviews with the participants showed that women with higher levels of testosterone chose riskier careers as their first jobs upon graduation—specifically, in finance.

While testosterone has previously been studied and found to have some correlation with competitiveness, gambling, and other male-dominant, high-stakes behaviors, the University of Chicago researchers' study appears to be the first investigation into the relationship between testosterone and financial risk-taking. [http://www.forbes.com/2009/08/25/risk-finance-testosterone-forbes-woman-leadership-behavior.html] Its implications go beyond the results noted above, which portray women's correlations between testosterone and risk-related behavior. This study also has interesting implications about men as compared to women. In the study, just 36 per cent of the female students chose high-risk financial careers such as investment banking or trading, compared to 57 per cent of male students. "In general, women are more risk-averse than men when it comes to making important financial decisions, which in turn can affect their career choices," states Paola Sapienza, one of the study's authors. Another member of the team, Luigi Zingales, states: "This study has significant implications for how the effects of testosterone could impact on actual risk-taking in financial markets, because many of these students will go on to become major players in the financial world." In short, people with higher levels of testosterone seem more likely to pursue risky careers in business and finance. While earlier studies have shown that people with high testosterone levels are generally more competitive and dominant, this is the first time the hormone has been proven to have specific impacts on career choice. http://www.independent.co.uk/news/science/ruthless-women-have-extra-testosterone-scientists-show-1776769.html]

Can we draw a conclusion from this research that testosterone levels are the *sole* determinant of career choice? Of course not. Does it indicate that testosterone levels are a *significant* determinant of career choice? Perhaps. But career choice doesn't *in and of itself* determine career success. Both men and women with relatively high levels of testosterone have a variety of career options available; it's hard to believe that higher testosterone levels would *always* lead to high-risk careers.

More likely is the possibility that testosterone can *influence* certain kinds of behaviors within a given career. Within the business realm, perhaps it encourages a propensity for a relatively high degree of risk in making decisions. This conclusion seems closer to plausibility. (And of course aside from issues of risk as such, there are good decisions as well as bad decisions.) It's also possible that while the influence of testosterone varies from person to person, it may account (in part) for male executives' behaviors in many workplaces, including the corporate sphere.

(It may also suggest *one* reason why men have tended to excel in top management, where risk-taking is a necessary component of success. But it's also worth noting that the male-dominated business culture tends to reward competitiveness and risk-taking to a high degree—and these characteristics aren't necessarily factors in *successful* business behaviors; they are simply one model. And unless good risk-taking leads to good business decisions and effective implementation, risk-taking as such isn't useful. In fact, the lack of checks and balances in the banking and financial sectors in recent years may well be a case of extreme and unchecked risk-taking.)

Regardless of these various issues, it seems premature to assume that one single factor—that is, a higher or lower level of a single hormone—accounts for all the complexities and subtleties of choice for executives, much less for all human beings. There's definitely far more to our life equation than our endocrine system. As Dr. James M. Dabbs, states: "To understand human nature, it is imperative to understand both biologic and social forces." But he also notes that "Behavioral or biological approaches are incomplete . . . Testosterone affects behavior, but the outcome of behavior also affects testosterone levels." Anne Fausto-Sterling, a geneticist and the author of *Myths of Gender*, notes what's problematic in attempts to correlate our behavior with a single hormonal state. "It's easy to forget that our bodies have a number of different hormonal systems, all of which interact with each other," she writes. "To attribute a change in behavior to a change in a single hormone, when many different hormones rise and fall simultaneously, misrepresents the actual physiological events."

So if other physiological factors need to be considered, what would those be? This question brings us to one of the most intriguing, complex, and controversial aspects of our inquiry.

Other Factors: Neuroanatomy and Neurophysiology

Sigmund Freud wrote famously—or infamously, in the view of most women—that "anatomy is destiny." By this he seems to have meant that the differences between men's and women's anatomical structures, including their reproductive organs, are a major determinant in their fates throughout life. Many observers and commentators (women especially, but men as well) have rightly rejected this opinion as determinist and sexist. But what if Freud were partly right? And what if the anatomical differences that matter most aren't the ones between the legs but, rather, those between the ears? In short, what if the neurological differences between male and female have a major impact on how men and women think, feel, and act?

Recent research into neuroanatomy and neurophysiology has fascinating implications for the differences between men and women. Specifically, certain neurological issues—such as aspects of how the brain is structured differently in the male brain compared to the female brain—appear to influence how men and women perform differently in significant ways. And some of these differences may offer clues about what happens in the corporate world as men and women pursue their careers.

Based on recent research, here are some interesting discoveries about those differences:

- The brain centers for language and hearing in women's brains have 11% more neurons than in men's brains.
- In women's brains compared to men's, psychological stress from conflict registers more deeply.
- Men have two and a half times the brain space devoted to sex drive compared to the equivalent area in women.
- Men also have larger processors at the core of the amygdala, the most primitive area of the brain, which registers fear and triggers aggression.
- Men and women have different brain sensitivities to stress and conflict.
- Men and women also use different brain areas and circuits to solve problems, process language, and experience and store strong emotion.
- The female and male brains process stimuli derived from hearing, seeing, sensing, and gauging what others are feeling in different ways. [Louann Brisendine, *The Female Brain*, pp. 4-6.]

These and many other fascinating observations appear in Louann Brisendine's recent book, *The Female Brain*, which describes this scientist's view of how male and female neuroanatomy and neurophysiology affect how men and women experience and respond to the world. This book—as well as Brisendine's companion volume, *The Male Brain*—offer a fascinating array of opinions about how we are all hardwired in gender-specific ways. As I'll note shortly, there are significant drawbacks to any interpretation that regards these physiological issues *as a complete explanation*; however, research into the differences between men's and women's brains is remarkable and deserves close attention. These issues may also shed light on how male and female executives perform in the business world. As Dr. Brisendine summarizes the situation: "These basic, structural variances in [male and female] brains lay groundwork for many everyday differences between the behavior and life experiences of men and women."

By now you may be saying, "Well, this is all very interesting—but what does it have to do with women in a corporate setting?" I believe that current research in neuroscience has some interesting answers to this question. What Dr. Brisendine and others have to say on this topic, for instance, suggests that the differing natures of men's and women's brains may significantly influence what happens between men and women, including in the board room. The male brain seems hardwired (as Dr. Brisendine states) to thrive under competition, to prompt instinctive "rough play," and to be obsessed with rank and hierarchy. The female brain, meanwhile, is "a lean, mean communication machine" that thrives best in the midst of complex, subtle relationships—unlike the male brain, which generally tends not to track the intricacies of personal interactions so closely. It's not hard to imagine how these different predispositions would affect life in upper management. If nothing else, the situation will put outnumbered women at a disadvantage in coping with their male peers. And especially since men have had a centuries-long head start in setting the rules in the business world, it's not hard to see how women may find frustrating an arena that neither understands nor values their unique skill set.

But anatomy and physiology aren't the whole story. Neurons may be the "hard wiring," but human beings, like computers, also have software—the programming that runs on the hardware.

Rank and hierarchy, for instance, aren't simply (or solely) hard-wired male characteristics. They are also aspects of male organizational models driven by male-centric preferences. It's true that any organization needs a structure of some sort; otherwise work cannot be performed efficiently and effectively. For these reasons, rank and hierarchy aren't inherently bad. What may constrain women is instead a set of hierarchical rules that are one-sided. Left to their own devices, women might well devise a structure that includes rules for rank and hierarchy . . . but the rules would probably be different from men's rules. What I'm describing here is just one example of what we could call the "software"—the programming—of the human "hardware." And this point brings us necessarily to the issue of culture.

THE PLOT THICKENS: CULTURE AND ITS EFFECTS

Listen to these two stereotypes—keeping in mind that these are, in fact, stereotypes:

- Members of one gender are quick to show their emotions. They are perceived as intense but not very dependable. They are sensitive and have well-developed intuition, and in many cases are not expected to be very logical. They are comfortable embracing one another and sometimes hold hands in public.
- Members of the other gender are, by contrast, perceived as logical and coldly practical. They are less emotional than the other gender. In many situations, they can be quite ruthless.

Which gender is which? *Again, keeping in mind that these are stereotypes,* most Americans would be more likely to say that women fit the first stereotype; men are more likely to fit the second. But in Iran, assumptions about the stereotypes would tend to run just the opposite pattern. Iranians more often perceive men as emotionally intense, intuitive, and unreliable, while they are more likely to perceive women as practical and exhibiting a more rational bent.

[Pam Haley, DBHS Social Anthropology, or the http://socialanthropology2009-10.blogspot.com/2009/08/excerpts-from-edward-t-hall.html]

Well, you say, these are just stereotypes. True. But stereotypes tell us something—and the fact that these American and Iranian stereotypes about men and women are essentially polar opposites tells us, among other things, that culture has enormous influence on how we perceive individuals. It's not solely brain anatomy and physiology that call the shots. Although nature clearly has great influence on how human beings function, nurture does, too. The impact of nurture—a culture's assumptions, values, expectations, and mores—will affect what individuals can do . . . including what they can do in the business realm.

Here's another example. Like many or most women in this country, I find that American men often don't express their emotions. This is one of the most common complaints that American women make about their husbands, boyfriends, brothers, sons, and male friends. Louann Brisendine and other neuroscientists would probably state that this gap in emotional expressiveness between men and women is a direct result of differences in male and female neuroanatomy and neurophysiology. And maybe it is—in part. However, almost as soon as you take a look at communication in other cultures, this situation begins to look much more complicated. A male Mexican-American friend tells me, for instance, that men in Latino societies are much more expressive of their feelings, and expressions of this sort are culturally accepted and expected. Non-Latino travelers to Mexico and other Latin countries often remark on how emotional the men there seem—including emotional expression of sorts that would be looked down on in U.S. culture, such as crying in public. According to my Mexican-American friend, Latino men in turn are often amazed and exasperated by how inexpressive and buttoned-down American males seem. "We call them *hombres de hielo*," he says—"men of ice" or "ice men." I have read similar descriptions quoting men from some African nations, some Middle Eastern men, and males of other cultures who are baffled by how minimally their American brethren express their feelings. In short, even some supposedly hard-wired factors, such as emotion, aren't so hardwired after all; they are heavily influenced by culture. What American women may regard as the "nature" of men may be partly just a consequence of nurture and how behavior gets shaped in one culture as compared to another.

Here's why this issue is important: once again it tells us that so many of the attributes in the business world that people try to explain as externally determined are, in fact, culturally influenced. They are *structures* that have been created and left in place. They aren't the result of the "nature" of things so much as the result of decisions and assumptions made over a period of generations that foster a society's ability to function in agreed-upon ways. But these ways aren't "hardwired." Quite the contrary: they are most often *programmed* . . . not "programmed" in some pre-planned way, but rather by means of the ordinary teaching and fostering of values that goes on when parents raise their children. And no matter what we claim, parental expectations toward girls and boys often differ. They differ dramatically in traditional cultures, and they differ even in cultures like ours, which

A New Paradigm for Ambitious Women

are relatively egalitarian toward the sexes. Here's an example. While parents frequently encourage boys to be more assertive—even aggressive—in many situations (the classroom, the playing field, and a variety of social settings), parents may expect girls to be less "pushy" in these same arenas. The overall situation has changed in recent decades; the era of Victorian expectations about "ladylike" behavior are long over. However, old attitudes die hard. Some vestiges of old attitudes may still foster forthright behavior among boys and men, perhaps leading to males rising higher in the corporate hierarchy.

It should come as no surprise to any woman who has worked in the business world that most of the current structures, rules, and values in the corporate world are male-defined and male-driven. Many of these structures, rules, and values leave women at a disadvantage. While the wider culture may account for many aspects of expectations within the corporate world, it's also true that companies differ from one another. Some companies are more hospitable to women than others are—something I witnessed first hand throughout my own career. However, almost all companies put women at a disadvantage as female executives try to work their way up the corporate ladder. The core issue here isn't just the "male model"—it's that *we don't even bother to identify the model, much less question the model.* That is, we all follow the rules without recognizing that there are rules—and without admitting that the rules are male-defined, male-driven, and male-centric.

Here is an interesting comparison: the number of women in the Swedish Parliament compared to the number of women in the U.S. Congress. "The newly elected Swedish parliament is the most gender-balanced in its history," according to an article in *The Local,* a Swedish English-language newspaper and website. This article goes on to state that "When the new Riksdag [parliament] meets for the first time on October 2nd, women will be better represented than ever. Of the 349 parliament members, 47 percent are women (164 people)." [New Swedish parliament 'most gender-balanced ever' 22 Sep 09, http://www.thelocal.se/4996/20060922/] And the gender balance in the U.S. Congress? According to an article in the *Wikipedia*, "As of 2009, 441 members of Congress are male (83%) and 92 are female (17%). Some people may respond to these numbers and note that Scandinavia has a long history of feminism and of affirmative action for women. However, this issue begs the question. Sweden is, in fact, only the second most gender-balanced parliament in the world. The country in first place: Rwanda, where 48.8 percent of representatives are women, according to the Inter-Parliamentary Union. [http://en.wikipedia.org/wiki/Members_of_the_111th_United_States_Congress]

Even if the United States lags far behind Scandinavia and parts of central Africa in the numbers of women in government, it's also true that our country has made significant progress in other professions. Take, for instance, the medical profession: "The number of women practicing medicine in the United States has grown steadily since the late 1960s, with women now roughly at parity with men among entering medical students." [Review of *The Changing Face of Medicine: Women Doctors and the Evolution of Health Care in America*, by Ann K. Boulis and Jerry A. Jacobs: http://www.cornellpress.cornell.edu/cup_detail.taf?ti_id=5252] Consider also the legal professions, where women are now extensively represented. 29.1% of all lawyers in the United States are women. (Source: ABA Marketing Research, National Lawyer Population Survey Statistics, 2003). Women comprise 45.34% of associates at large law firms and 18.74% of partners at large law firms (Source: 2008-2009 NALP Directory of Legal Employers). Among women employed in law schools, they are 19.8% of deans, 29.3% of full professors, 46.8%

of associate professors, and 43.9% of assistant professors (Source: 2007-2008 AALS Statistical Report on Law Faculty) [Data from "Women in the legal profession," courtesy of the Stanford Center on the Legal Profession: http://womenlaw.stanford.edu/statistics.html}. Employment statistics continue to reflect gains by women in many sectors. In fact, women make up very nearly 50% of the American workforce. [*The Economist*, 2 January 2010, page 49.]

What I'm suggesting through all these statistics is essentially as follows. For centuries, men excluded women from most professions. The rationales differed, but they often stressed women's unsuitability, incompetence, moodiness, or outright inability to do the work. Women were "too flighty," "too delicate," "too emotional," or "too unpredictable" to do surgery, practice law, run a government, fly a plane, or—fill in the blank. More recently, women have gained opportunities to prove otherwise. We have excelled in every field. Women now swell the ranks of most of the professions. One unfortunate exception, however, is the upper reaches of many organizations—not only corporate management but also in almost any other organizations where a hierarchy exists. As we've noted already, the numbers for women in the C Suite are deplorable. I simply don't believe that the so-called "hard wiring" issue would explain this situation.

Presumably, the men in these other countries have brains that are anatomically and physiologically the same as the brains of American men. Likewise, the women in other countries have brains that are anatomically and physiologically the same as the brains of American women. Neuroscientists and others who, like Louann Brisendine, stress the primacy of nature over nurture, can't persuasively claim that "hard wiring" explains such dramatic differences in the levels of representation by men and women in, say, the United States compared to Iceland. Other factors are clearly at the root of these differences.

The remarkable difference in representation is clearly not a result of biological factors; rather, it is an expression of culture. The implication: if we're going to redress the imbalance in the number of women in upper management, it's not necessary to delve more deeply into the issues of biology. The core issue is, in fact, the cultural assumptions about women and how those assumptions limit women in the business hierarchy.

Now let's have a look at how biology and corporate culture add up—or, more accurately—don't.

AT THE INTERSECTION OF NATURE AND NURTURE: CHILDBEARING

The last time I checked, women were the people bearing all the babies. So, yes, childbearing is a biological reality for women. This is certainly one situation where "hard wiring" will explain who's doing what. I'll wager top dollar that it's women who will be giving birth to all the babies for at least the foreseeable future.

Where does this leave us in the corporate world? By necessity, women must take time off from work for childbearing and for the earliest phases of parenting. Corporate America has made some concessions—though often grudgingly—to this biological reality. Yes, maternity leave is available for most female executives. However, the sad truth is that taking advantage of these options will imperil many women's careers. While a company may grant a female officer time off for childbearing and childrearing, the very act of taking maternity leave may damage her career. Why? Because she may be consigning herself to "the Mommy Track"; her peers and superiors may regard her as less ambitious, less aggressive, or less committed to a straight-and-narrow career path. Often, the impact of her absence for childbearing and family isn't evident until later in her career, but the stage is set the moment she becomes pregnant. But it's worth stressing right off that this supposedly "biological" dimension of the problem really isn't biological at all. This set of issues isn't really about having babies; rather, it's about how the corporate world perceives *women's career paths* in relation to *men's career paths*—and how corporations then find women's career decisions "wanting" in comparison to this pre-determined standard. Strict and unforgiving adherence to a linear career is one of the most deadly career killers for women.

I've coped with these issues first hand, including all of the work/life balance issues that most women face, struggle with, and discuss every year in scores of newspaper and magazine articles and on thousands of web sites. Later in this book, I'll share stories from my own experiences that I believe shed light on the complex dimensions of this situation. I want to sidestep my own personal past for a moment, though, to focus on another aspect of the concepts we're discussing.

WOMEN'S QUANDARY: SUPPORT AND AMBITION

In this chapter so far, we've looked at factors that influence women's behavior and success (or lack of success) in the workplace. We have a clearer understanding now of the physiological differences and cultural differences that "frame" a woman's entry into the business place. But once she completes her education and begins her career, she'll start off just like the guys, right? Isn't it true that in our more enlightened era, we women and our male peers enter the workplace with the same set of ambitions and expectations for success? Not so fast. Some interesting new studies suggest that women and their ambitions don't encounter what men and their ambitions do.

Liberty and Justice for Her?

Here's what concerns me.

Achievement (mastery) and recognition (affirmation) are two elements necessary for a person's attainment of excellence throughout his or her education. In my view, what's most important about this situation is that the need for recognition extends throughout a man's or a woman's career and life. A lack of recognition may result in an individual feeling "it's just not worth it" to pursue continually more difficult and challenging roles in the workforce. And this long-term impact is significant because of research strongly suggesting that girls and women are recognized differently and to a lesser degree than is true for boys and men.

In my mind, the most worrisome evidence comes from studies that demonstrate how from childhood on, women's lives are filled with a sequence of experiences in which other people (chiefly parents and teachers) encourage in girls a quiet withdrawal and the ceding of available attention to others, particularly in the presence of men. A *Harvard Business Review* article by Anna Fels titled "Do Women Lack Ambition?" [*HBR*, April 2004] outlines these issues in disturbing detail. Dr. Fels notes that in contrast to what girls and women experience, boys and young men are generally recognized and rewarded (whether overtly or subtly) more than is true for girls and women. [Fels, p. 54.] By contrast, girls and women are often rewarded for self-effacing, self-denying, or other-oriented behaviors. What accounts for this pattern of encouraging deferential behavior in girls and women? To some extent it may be a culture-wide assumption that such behavior is "natural." But this assumption doesn't hold up to close scrutiny. As Anna Fels notes, when women compete with each other, they do so completely. Ceding recognition and reward isn't "natural" to women; on the contrary, it is "programmed" into girls and women in relation to men from an early age. One result is that when competing with men, girls' and women's behavior changes dramatically: they tend to defer, thus shunning the recognition that is a driver (and often a predictor) of success.

An informative portrait of these behaviors comes to us by means of the Bem Sex Role Inventory, or BSRI. This is an empirical instrument (a questionnaire) that social scientists use to study issues of gender. First used to study male and female Stanford University undergraduates in the 1970s, the BSRI ranks how respondents perceive the desirability of a wide range of "feminine" and "masculine" personality traits in American society. Traits identified as "feminine" in this questionnaire are: yielding, loyal, cheerful, compassionate, shy, sympathetic, affectionate, sensitive to the needs of others, responsive to flattery, understanding, eager to soothe hurt feelings, soft-spoken, warm, tender, gullible, childlike, unwilling to use harsh language, loving toward children, and gentle. Even a cursory review of these attributes reveals two basic assumptions about femininity. The first is a perception that femininity exists chiefly or solely in the context of relationships. That is, a woman's femininity is based on qualities expressed not in isolation but in relation to other people. A second assumption evident in these findings is that a woman must *provide* in some way for other people; giving is an activity or attribute that significantly defines femininity. By contrast, "masculine" traits are defined neither by relationships nor by what men provide to others—except in providing financially. The adjectives in the BSRI that described masculinity are: self-reliant, strong personality, forceful, independent, analytical, defends one's beliefs, athletic, assertive, has leadership abilities, willing to take risks, makes decisions easily, self-sufficient, dominant, willing to take a stand, aggressive, acts as a leader, individualistic, competitive, ambitious. The implications are that men can be masculine primarily *in isolation,* not in relation to others.

I find it interesting that in the years since social scientists first started using this instrument, college women in various studies have demonstrated more "masculine" traits than was true in the past—but they haven't necessarily dropped any of the "feminine" traits along the way. For instance, recent female respondents have endorsed goals such as becoming an authority figure, obtaining recognition from colleagues, having administered to responsibilities, and being better off financially. Yet in the wider world, women's attainment of greater access to social influence and recognition (such as legal and political rights, educational opportunities and career options) hasn't spared them from criticism that they are less fully "real women" than in the past. In short, women may have disengaged from culturally determined biases about femininity yet paid a price in terms of criticism and derision for being less feminine as a result.

What concerns me most in the context of our current discussion, however, is that both in the past and currently, the BSRI instrument shows interesting and disturbing patterns about how our culture defines femininity and masculinity:

> *Femininity is described primarily or only in terms of a relationship and of giving something to others.*
>
> *Masculinity is not defined by relationships or by a context in which giving to others is a primary value.*
>
> *Thus, being "feminine" is fundamentally a support role, while being "masculine" is fundamentally a role of standing alone and/or of being supported.*

The implications are deeply troubling. Women can receive the same training and learning; they can have the same job experience; they can participate in the same meetings and interactions as men in their workplace. But if femininity is perceived chiefly in terms of *being supportive of others,* and if masculinity doesn't include similar attributes of supportiveness toward others—including women—then women in the workplace are inherently at a disadvantage. They will be putting an inordinate amount of time and effort into offering support to people around them, including their male peers, who probably outnumber them in the first place. They will also be receiving less practical and emotional support from others, since their male peers aren't likely to see supportiveness as one of their own attributes and obligations, much less as a fundamental dimension of their role as men. Where does this situation leave women? In many contexts, it means that if women aren't directly and indirectly recognized and rewarded in ways that are similar to those for men, they will be at a significant disadvantage as they try to thrive and grow. Their ambitions will be constrained—and perhaps even significantly thwarted.

Perhaps not ironically, this quandary will probably become most challenging during what is often the most stressful time of a woman's life: the childbearing years. Just when a woman is new to the workplace and perhaps also new to early stages of her marriage, she must decide whether or not to curb her ambitions to "have it all." By now the culture has taught her well. She can only have it all if she first sees to the needs of spouse, child, perhaps extended family, while taking care not to cause a ripple in the workplace. And she must accomplish all of these goals in the face of less recognition and reward than what many male peers receive. All too often, it may be just too easy to throttle back on the career or to put it off until later.

Liberty and Justice for Her?

WHAT SEEMS TO HELP... BUT OFTEN DOESN'T

As you read over what I've written about women's ambitions and the issues that obstruct career advancement, you may be thinking, "Okay, all of this sounds true enough. But aren't there programs in place throughout the corporate world that help to address these problems? What about all the diversity and inclusion initiatives?" That's a valid point. Many companies have made good-faith efforts to level the playing field for women. However, I believe that many of these programs are problematic either by *seeming* to address the issues without necessarily helping at all; or else these factors can actually make matters worse.

I want to begin by stating outright that these programs—and the affirmative action programs that preceded them during the 1970's and 1980's—have unquestionably done much to advance women's careers in many sectors. I was the diversity and inclusion officer during some of my years at Texas Instruments, and I did as much as possible to foster the careers of women and minorities in each of my careers. So, as you can imagine, I certainly see the value of these programs. I believe, however, that diversity and inclusion programs are a double-edged sword. While they have advanced the standing of many individual women and minorities within the business world, they have also complicated the tasks facing women executives as they try to climb the corporate ladder. What I'm describing is especially true for women in the upper reaches of management.

Here's why.

Let me start with a couple of personal stories. My own experiences with the diversity and inclusion movement have been complex and often intense. The first ten to fifteen years of changes were all about affirmative action. This approach created opportunities for women, but it also generated plenty of resentment throughout the corporate world. In my own situation at TI in those days, I ended up in an incredibly awkward position. As the diversity and inclusion phase started up, the men I worked with often said things like, "Connie, I didn't know you felt like that." They use those words—"felt like that"—because diversity and inclusion *assumed* that women were significantly dissatisfied with their status, and need "extra help" to fit in. Likewise, men also had to go through training to learn to be more inclusive. Because of diversity and inclusion, my male colleagues now concluded that I must also be dissatisfied. Most importantly, some felt that I had not been truthful over the years. It was a lose/lose circumstance. As I noted in Chapter 1, I had made every effort to blend in. Now I was denying that I was ever really satisfied? The situation was terribly awkward.

It's true that to some degree, the growing presence of women in the corporate world—including in upper management—required men to adjust to situations that were unfamiliar and sometimes threatening to them. I have a vivid memory of when, as only the second female vice president at Texas Instruments, I stopped reporting to my earlier boss and reported instead to two line managers. One of them was a man who literally wouldn't look me in the eye during my initial interview. Definitely a warning sign! I told myself, "Don't take this job." But I did. I had many difficult times interacting with both of those male line managers. Fortunately, my mentor at the time backed me completely in every way. But regardless, my progress was often an uphill battle. The effort became even more difficult when I was appointed the first diversity manager for TI. At one meeting, a male executive came up to me and unloaded furiously about the diversity program I was leading. "I'm not about to let you bring down this company!" he shouted. I was deeply hurt and angered by this interchange. Deep down I knew he was just taking his anger and frustration out on the messenger. But I also knew that I was now being painted with a different brush. I was no longer one of the guys, and I knew that my career would be forever colored by these circumstances. The truth was, I'd simply been appointed to that position—perhaps because I was the only senior woman available—and I, like any woman involved in the process at the time, suffered a degree of guilt by association in the eyes of many men. Worse, I knew I had lost the innate trust of many senior men that I had worked so hard to build over the years. I believe that this dichotomy is the fundamental reason senior level women tend to not take a strong, proactive role with regards to the careers of other women. Rather, everyone just assumes that if you put the "right mechanisms in place," positive change will occur over time. We now know this is not the case.

Moving beyond my personal experiences to the bigger picture, here's how I see the situation. Most companies are serious about diversity and inclusion training, and they spend a lot of money on this approach. It's clear that the overall intentions of the people involved in these programs are good, and that many benefits have been realized. However, I believe that unless we look at the situation from a wider perspective, we in the corporate world may be missing some crucial issues. With respect to women, here are some questions I feel we need to ask:

- What are these programs' goals? Are the goals to help everyone feel good about diversity and inclusion, or actually to foster real change?

- Who is accountable for reaching these goals? And how will the goals be documented and measured?
- How do diversity and inclusion training programs impact pay—and how is that impact linked to performance management systems? (At lower levels within the corporate setting, the outcomes from diversity and inclusion programs are better documented; higher up on the corporate ladder, the cause-effect relationships aren't so clear.)

My fundamental concern is whether these programs will lead to equity in pay and position. To the degree that there's been genuine change, it has occurred chiefly for women and minorities in the lower and middle ranks of management. This is a significant achievement. However, it's not at all clear there will be commensurate changes at the senior levels of management. So far, this definitely has not happened. The numbers for women in the C Suite remain stagnant at about 16% despite many years of programs supposedly designed to foster the upward progress of female executives.

Here are the specific focal points of my concern.

These programs are well intentioned but only go so far

At their worst, diversity and inclusion programs are essentially just "window dressing" approaches that don't really produce any measurable results. They do allow a company to point and say, "Look at all the progressive things we're doing." They all about embracing and valuing "differences." The underlying theme is: "Since we now have women in the workplace, we must take time away from real work to insure that everyone feels valued and is included." Unfortunately, this approach doesn't actually change the criteria for success in most corporations.

They create a disparity between "the ideal" and "the real"

What I mean in the preceding commentary is this: there's a real gap between the values and understandings promoted in diversity and inclusion programs and the measuring sticks that are central to life in upper management. What are the most important characteristics of executives? The Center for Creative Leadership reports on interviews with 200,000 respondents regarding what they see as executives' most valuable skills and perspectives. 87% of respondents state that the most valuable skill for executives is "leading employees." At the bottom are issues like "career management," "respecting individual differences," "compassion," and "sensitivity." The reality of the business world is all about producing results. The "softer" stuff is important, but the higher you go up the ladder, the more it's all about the numbers. This isn't a bad thing. But if women are learning different "values" in diversity and inclusion training, they may be led to think the company places a higher value on certain things *when in reality they don't*. Right away, we can see that there's a disparity between what the diversity and inclusion programs advocate compared to what executives actually value and how they behave. This is a fundamental issue in its own right.

Here's a further reality check. An outplacement company that I've interacted with describes the image that an executive *must* project when actively looking for a job. According to this firm's approach, a strong executive must present this "message": "I am a professional, I have no problems, I will present no problems, and I will help you solve your problems." If this is the image central to being an executive, then there's an inherent gap between this persona and the one that diversity and inclusion programs stress as acceptable and permissible. What is that other persona? It's the notion that a female or minority executive needs special treatment, requires special conditions to thrive, and requests or demands adaptations to current protocols or executive roles. This persona will not help you gain entry into the C Suite.

These programs may foster isolation rather than inclusion and advancement

As a result of what I'm describing, such programs—which in the past might well have been a bridge to equality—may now become islands where women end up isolated . . . and wondering how on earth they got there. These programs accommodate women by offering flex schedules, formal mentoring programs, and other adjustments. That's good, right? Well, yes, to some degree. But this approach also reinforces the mindset that some (or all) women need a different measuring stick to succeed—or that they need "extra" help to do what otherwise committed, loyal employees (i.e., men) need. What I'm describing often results in a backlash from male executives, and this backlash can completely undo the gains that the programs themselves might have yielded. Men who may have equal needs less often take advantage of such programs (and, in the case of options like paternity leave, rarely take them at all), thus continuing the image of the strong, rugged, independent male. Is this situation a women's fault? Of course not. But it's a situation that female executives face, and it's a serious problem that may significantly confound their efforts to advance.

These programs may undercut honesty and trust between men and women

The worst aspect of diversity and inclusion programs is that they may break down the honesty and trust between men and women that are so vital to success at the top. If men (and some women) resent time spent in diversity training, the situation can backfire. Why? Because women feel may guilty about needing special attention and treatment, while men simultaneously resent the time spent in an activity they may deem useless.

These programs may distract us from the real changes that are necessary

Finally, there's a contributing element that stems from the notion of accommodation (or inclusion): how do we accommodate (include) *women?* But this situation tends to focus on the wrong aspects of accommodation. It essentially reflects a question: "How do we fit B into an A-shaped structure?" The assumption is that "A"—being male—is the proper structure . . . so if you are "B"—female—your presence is a problem to be solved. This is the wrong question. When we ask it, female executives find themselves by implication *defined* as out of place—as players who need to be "accommodated." The most successful women execs are those who have "adapted" successfully to the male model. This situation is inherently problematic. The more important question (at least in my mind) should be: How do we create a structure in which both men and women fit effectively and can work creatively?

ASSUMPTIONS— AND CONSEQUENCES

Throughout this chapter, I've tried to describe what women are up against and how so many of the obstacles we face are the result of *assumptions* about women rather than any *fundamental aspect* of women's "nature." I would be the first to state that none of what I've described here is radically new. Even most men in the corporate world would accept the fact that there's nothing innate in women that prevents them from serving productively and creatively in the C Suite. I don't believe that individual men are really the core barrier that women confront. Rather, the fundamental problem is a set of assumptions—often unstated assumptions—that I've referred to earlier as "the boys rules." Precisely because the guys have always played by these rules, and because they take them for granted, they don't necessarily even perceive them. Women, by contrast, face them from the outside, don't necessarily see them clearly or understand them fully, and thus face major problems in coping with them, trying to play by them successfully, or attempting to change them into something more fair and effective for everyone. Diversity and inclusion programs may seem to address these problems, but I don't believe they do so productively. To some degree, these programs often backfire or complicate women's careers rather than smoothing out the path ahead.

Which probably leaves you muttering, "Okay, great. The situation is a real mess. So tell me this, Connie: what are we supposed to do about it?"

That's what the rest of this book is about.

CHAPTER 3

THE BURDEN OF ISOLATION

Years ago, when I became a vice president at Texas Instruments, I attended my first senior executive leadership meetings at that company. In attendance were all the other vice presidents and senior officers—almost 200 people. I was only the second female vice president at TI, so just two women were present. She and I were outnumbered by men at a ratio of almost 100 to one! To this day, I can remember vividly how insignificant and alone I felt at that first meeting. But the male-to-female ratio as such wasn't really the source of my discomfort. What troubled me far more was that during the course of that two- or three-day meeting, not even one of my fellow senior officers came up to congratulate me, welcome me, or acknowledge me in any other way. At break, for example, everyone else would go off into their groups to chat. I ventured over to a group at one point, and the men there were friendly enough, and some of them even tried to include me in the conversation, but it was so obvious that the tone had changed completely when I joined the group. I couldn't help but feel uncomfortable. It wasn't long before I simply stopped trying. This was not a pleasant experience! Nobody was actively excluding me—I simply wasn't even showing upon their radar screens. I felt as if I were on the outside looking in. And I was.

ISOLATION IS REALITY

It's true that the meeting I've described took place many decades ago. That was a time not only of very few female executives; there were also only minimal resources available for the handful of women who had risen into the managerial hierarchy. I could have benefited from many of the resources that are now routinely available. For instance, a coach would have been a huge help. A network also would have been a great benefit to me. I desperately needed someone to talk to; I had no one to go to. Even my mentor—who had promoted me and who backed me in many ways—wasn't someone I was comfortable approaching. I didn't want to whine or seem weak or ungrateful. It never crossed my mind to be angry or frustrated with the men. I missed a wonderful chance to do some learning, but I was too ashamed to admit my discomfort.

It's also true that despite the very significant gains for women over the ensuing years, Texas Instruments remains a very male-dominant work environment, as is true for many other technology companies. That situation made it easy for a woman to feel isolated. Later, in my other careers—especially during the time I spent at Cox Communications—I attained a much greater sense of connection with other executives. However, the situation I've described here contains a crucial reality that all women face in upper management. *The nature of being a female executive is to be isolated.* It's true that women are now less excluded at lower levels of many corporations. However, precisely because there are so few women at the upper rungs of the corporate ladder, we have few peers, whether male or female—and we often have no female peers at all. This situation is inherently problematic. The higher you go in the hierarchy, the more isolation you will experience. You'll have less information and less access, which in turn means you will be less advantaged as you perform your executive duties. The tighter the circles at the top, the more a person loses out when she isn't "in the circle."

The problem for women isn't just in the formal channels for exchanging information. Female executives may, in fact, have full access to those channels in most companies. Rather, the situation is more likely to lie in the informal settings for exchange of information—settings that men have put in place for generations and continue to use without a second thought. For instance, I referred earlier to golf as a setting for work-related socializing and discussion. Other sports, clubs, and any number of other traditional masculine activities and venues serve similar purposes. Women at the higher reaches of the corporate hierarchy may not be included in these activities and venues—or else they may be put in a position of feeling so uncomfortable as to remove themselves voluntarily. The result: a lack of access to the full flow of informal information among major players. This lack of information may be damaging, even crippling, to a female executive and to what she can accomplish day-to-day, month-to-month, and over the longer term during the course of her career. Additionally, *out of sight* equals *out of mind*. You are either a player or you're not.

I want to state outright that the situation isn't always black-and-white.

Even at Texas Instruments, which was a very macho environment, I felt included in some ways. As I came up through the organization,

I generally felt like part of the team even though very few women in that company were managers. Overall, I felt pretty good about my situation there. It's certainly possible that as a young woman starting a career, I may not have been critical enough or assertive enough. But at that point in time I was thankful simply to be there, and I just made it work. I didn't feel forcibly excluded. I saw that the rules were "the boys' rules," and I made a conscious decision to play—and win—by following those rules.

Later, during my time at Cox, many more women executives were present. For me, Cox, was probably the best of all worlds for a female executive. The sheer number of women present in middle and upper management was reassuring and exhilarating. In addition, there was an interchange between men and women, as well as high levels of energy that was totally different from what I had experienced at TI. When I had been with the company for only three weeks, for instance, I went to my first all-company senior management meeting. My boss took me around and introduced me to our colleagues. I felt an immediate and active sense of inclusion. Cox was a wonderful environment partly because of the sheer number of women present but also because of the collegiality among them, which was certainly a significant part of what made the environment so good. There was also a consciousness about women and open discussion of issues fostered by the most senior women there.

But did I still feel a sense of isolation at the upper levels of management? Here again, I have to be honest: sometimes, I did. Why? Because even to this day, there are still just a few women senior vice presidents at that company. About a third of their general managers were women—maybe six or seven. During my time at Cox, another issue was that a group known within the company as "The Big Eight"—the executives who ran most of the largest systems—were all men. It wasn't hard for a female executive to feel less connected and more out of the loop. It's also true that at Cox, as elsewhere, the overall numbers make a difference. If you are the only woman in a group of eight or ten executives, this ratio will affect not just how you feel emotionally but also what sort of power you wield within the group. And the reality of the corporate world is still power and influence.

Here's a personal experience that echoes in uncomfortable ways the story I told earlier about TI. Shortly after I became a GM at Cox, I was invited to go on a very exclusive trip to the Cannes film festival in France. Yes, Cox has a lot of female general managers—but I was the only woman present at that time among six or more of the larger division business heads. And the male executives—my peers—didn't speak to me. The trip in question was a junket, so there were no business meetings as such, just some structured and unstructured activities. Since the trip was for the execs and their spouses, my husband, Larry, had been invited to come along for the ride. On the third day I told him, "You know, these guys just aren't very friendly." Larry commented that the treatment I'd been getting was a real slap in the face. I still remember being embarrassed and somewhat shamed in front of my husband. Here I was, a brand-new woman exec on my first exclusive business trip . . . yet the guys wouldn't acknowledge or speak to me? In fairness, I should mention that there was a male who also wasn't included by the group. He and I spent a little time together, and he shared with me at that time that he just didn't hang around with them much. Whether this was his choice or not, I never knew. But the guys that hung out together were the movers and shakers, and I was excluded from the group. This trip could have been a wonderful opportunity for me to get to know my fellow-executives. But after about the second or third day, I realized that none of them showed any interest in getting to know me. Larry and I went off and did our own thing. Then, on the last night in Cannes, one of them came up to me and said, "You know, I'm really sorry we didn't have more time to talk during this trip. Sometime we'll have to do that." That comment was even more humiliating than the almost total lack of communication. It told me that they *did* notice me—but they had still declined to include me in any way at all.

Why is this so important? It wasn't just the social snub. Nobody likes to be left out, but I can live with that. The bigger problem—a very serious problem—is that if you are excluded from the ordinary give-and-take of a group, you miss out on the information and know-how that's part of the group's currency. And this issue is an especially acute problem for women in the corporate world. Female executives may have access to the formal channels for exchanging information, but they also need access to the informal systems. Exchanging information in the corporate world depends upon (and has always depended upon) long-standing male channels and rituals. These include mainstays such as golf, outdoor activities, and social clubs. Traditionally, women have been denied access to these channels. As in my case, you may be excluded even if you are present. Later on, I did get to know some of my peers from the Cannes trip, but it took a very long time for my resentment to cool. There were also two whom I never developed a relationship with. But the lack of formal barriers doesn't mean that women necessarily have full access to these channels. Often, exclusion is a result of women opting out because the situation is just too uncomfortable. (For instance, I've heard about women deciding not to join their male peers on a hunting trip because the lodge had only a single communal restroom.) The outcome is the same whether the means of exclusion is *de jure* or *de facto:* female executives aren't fully connected to their colleagues' informational network. I remember a time at TI when the plan for an Outward Bound excursion for our team was rejected because I was the only female who would have participated. The other team members were afraid that the multiday trip would be inappropriate for a woman. Because of this attitude, I was the sole reason the trip never happened. This decision not only sent a message to me; it also sent a message to my peers. The truth is, I was in great physical shape at the time, and I thought this excursion was a great idea. But my boss's perception was that having one woman on a multi-day outdoor adventure "just wouldn't work."

So, if we accept that executive women are often isolated, what are the sources of this isolation? How do otherwise strong, successful women find themselves on the outside? Here are what I see as the main issues—as well as some suggestions about how to resolve them.

MEN DEFINED THE RULES AND THE CULTURE A LONG TIME AGO

Throughout my careers, I would often hear men talking on Monday morning about something that some of them had done over the weekend. The executives at the top are often personal friends as well as business associates. Day in, day out, these guys spend time together. They spend time together at work and often when at play. When you're at company functions, they may have a mutual familiarity that you don't share with them. More often than not, their spouses are in a clearly support role.

Now it's true that among women, the situation may be similar: "the girls" may have their own network. But this is exactly the problem. If there simply aren't equal numbers of men and women, the women end up being sidelined. Nobody *intends* for it to happen. In fact, some people—including men—may go to great lengths to prevent this process of sidelining. Yet it may happen anyway. A good example is hallway conversations. People are more likely to stop and chat with somebody they feel closer to than with somebody they feel less close to. In my own experience, someone would pass me in the hallway and ask, "How was your weekend?" Fine. But I wasn't surprised that interactions between male colleagues might be more substantive than these more casual inquiries. If a male exec happened to come down the hall, the question from another guy might be: "Hey, what's your take on that meeting?" And off they'd go to have their private chat.

Part of what we're talking about are notions of how you play "the game." Some of that has to do with the channels of information, while some of it has to do with kind of the rituals or the culture of the company. It's no secret that in most of the corporate world, men have set the rules and defined the culture for hundreds of years. The specific rules vary from place to place, of course. But what's even more powerful—and often more constricting for women—is that formal and informal structures govern what happens within an organization. The formal structures generally include specific, often well-defined policies, guidelines, and practices. The informal structures are more free-form. Women often find themselves "outside the circle" because so many organizational decisions and processes occur by means of the informal structures—structures in which there are few or no visible policies, guidelines, and practices. How can you "play by the rules" when those rules are unstated and invisible?

EQUALITY BEGINS AT HOME

Strong women are strong everywhere—in the home, in the office, in their relationships. Once a woman has taken control of her own life and found her sense of agency, she takes it with her everywhere. But here is a painful truth: if women don't have equitable relationships in their own personal lives, they are significantly less likely to attain equality in the executive hierarchy. There are two central issues here. One is just physical labor and time: since the woman is always the spouse who bears the children, and since she is often the more-supportive parent and the caretaker of the household, she may feel less available to make the corporate climb. She may have less energy. She may simply have less time. But more importantly, if she is always psychologically and emotionally the "support person" at home, it's going to be much more difficult to be the leader at work. If she and her husband or partner don't have a truly equitable relationship, how will she be able to demand the equivalent at work?

What I'm describing is a quandary in its own right. In addition, it's a situation that will lead inevitably to isolation. Why? Because if women don't have equitable relationships in their own personal lives, they won't know how to manage equality within the executive suite. Part of the issue is energy and time. A female executive will be so busy taking care of family because of an unequal relationship that she'll have less time and energy for her corporate work. But even more important is her confidence. If she checks her autonomy at the door of her own home, she is essentially leading a "double life." And that's an incredibly difficult way of life.

Here's personal example of this struggle. For many years my husband, Larry, wouldn't consider a move away from the Lubbock area. When TI offered me an executive job in Austin, I told Larry I just had to accept the offer. "We need to make the situation work." What followed was a really, really difficult time for us. Frankly, I'm surprised that we didn't end up divorced somewhere along the way. But we both worked through the situation, we had a series of very difficult discussions, and we eventually found room for compromise. One reason I love my husband is that he's such a strong person, and he feels that same way toward me. That said, the TI job in Austin required some very strenuous negotiations and lots of compromise. I have always appreciated my mother's advice for a successful marriage: If both you and your spouse give 150%, and if you're very lucky, your marriage should survive. While the role of "lead dog" in a marriage may change many times, the key issue is for both spouses to agree about who is the leader at any given time. And there should be equal amounts of give-and-take over the course of your marriage.

The bottom line: marital support is something that women in the corporate world must pay attention to. I believe that many of us don't do that; we either sell ourselves short or even completely ignore that part of our lives. This approach is courting disaster. Women *must* consider the big picture—and *must* take steps to foster their autonomy. Because these issues of equality, autonomy, and agency are so important, I'll devote all of Chapter 4 to exploring them.

WOMEN OFTEN DON'T—OR CAN'T—SUPPORT ONE ANOTHER

There's a common assumption that the people blocking female executives' careers are usually men. This may be true at times; however, sometimes it's *women* who are unsupportive of their female peers or who compete with them at the upper reaches of the corporate ladder. (This competition may occur differently from how women compete with men, but it's still competition.) There are many reasons for this phenomenon. One is the side effects of acculturation. We know, for instance, that young girls compete for the attention of young men. They dress to be recognized by men. Girls may not have the opportunity to experience certain kinds of female group bonding the way that men do. As a result, women may need to learn how to develop these relationships as adults. And, as I noted earlier, we also know that women may compete with each other but hold back from competing so directly with men. Absent these types of supportiveness, women may experience more isolation than they would have otherwise in upper management.

Here are some other aspects of non-supportiveness among women executives.

Female Competitiveness

A common gender stereotype in America is that males are competitive with one another—often ruthlessly so—while females are mutually supportive. However, we now know that women compete more directly with each other and tend to be more supportive and perhaps less competitive with men. There's no question that boys and men often revel in competition. It's also true that girls and women are often collaborative when they work or play together. However, these patterns of behavior aren't the whole story. From early childhood on, girls are fully capable of being competitive; the social structures of girls in elementary school, middle school, and high school include plenty of competitive elements; and aspects of competition are prominent in the adult spheres of work as well. It shouldn't be surprising that in corporate management, some women will compete just as intensely against one another as they do with their male colleagues. One aspect of this competitiveness may be a tendency for some female executives to hold back support from other women because they see them as a threat.

I believe that what women sometimes miss is the gamesmanship of competition. It is a sport in and of itself; it need not be personal.

The real question is whether you are competing within a team or against a team. If she is an "outsider," competition looks and feels different. If she "loses" a promotion or a big deal, she may not have the advantage of being supported and absorbed back into the group.

Senior Women Often Fall Silent about Other Women

Women at the most senior levels in corporations should be in a unique position to effect change at the top. However, some may feel that doing so will put them at risk. First of all, most senior women would agree that women's advancement isn't perceived as a "key business imperative"; that is, the lack of women at senior levels isn't seen as an element critical to the success of any individual corporation. Particularly in the short run, it would be detrimental for a senior woman to insist that the lack of other senior women should become a key focus of the corporation. It's true, however, that statistics show diverse companies having the best results for long-term value creation and sustainability. Yet the leadership teams of most major corporations aren't terribly diverse, and pushing for model-changing actions, accountability, and goals would likely be perceived as getting "off course"—or at least not as important as other key business imperatives. It would be a huge risk for any woman to advocate this approach—and, frankly, why should she take that risk?

This is an issue of political capital. Will a female executive expend time, energy, effort, and credibility to foster other women or to promote women's issues under circumstances where her chief goal is to meet her numbers and achieve the other goals that she's being pressured to do? For many, the pressure and time involved simply to meet business goals is all-encompassing. Fostering other women's careers may seem appealing in abstract but too big a gamble in practical terms. Supporting other women may be one of many efforts she pursues, but it never rises to the level of being one of the critical few business imperatives. Additionally, if the senior women are in support roles—such as Human Resources, Administration, or Public Relations—a female executive's status is even less secure. The "critical few" business imperatives are generally not the purview of support positions, but of Finance, Marketing, Sales or Engineering, all areas where women are less well-represented.

An Economy of Scarcity?

What I'm describing here about competition and vulnerability may prove all the more true when women see their corporate sphere as an economy of scarcity—and, more specifically, if they perceive one of the scarce "commodities" to be job advancement for women. That is, women may feel threatened by other women if the positions available to female executives are perceived as severely limited. (Social scients define *economy of scarcity* as a culture—in this case, a corporate culture—in which resources are perceived as so limited that any person's gain will be regarded as someone else's loss.) If a company is likely to promote only a few women into higher levels of management, then each woman is a threat to the other women's chances for advancement. One result of this situation may be a reluctance by female executives to support each other: to share information, to give each other breaks, to form alliances, to share power, and to do any of the many other things that can boost someone else's career.

The Curse of "The Girls' Team"

Despite all the excellence in women's athletics visible in the world of sports, there remains a bias in many sectors against "the girls' team." The real action (and the big money) is when the guys are playing!

Something similar to this bias may spill over into the corporate world. No matter how well women executives may excel, there's a common tendency to assume that what matters most is what the *men* are doing. As a result of this phenomenon, some women may be reluctant to forge alliances with their female peers because it is not where the "action" is.

Worries about Being Stigmatized

As I stated in Chapter 2, diversity and inclusion programs have advanced the careers of many women. One side effect of these programs, however, is that some female executives may worry that others perceive their advancement as the direct result of these programs—and, worse yet, people may perceive promotions as being based on affirmative action (by whatever name) rather than on merit alone. The risk is of being stigmatized. When I interviewed the CEO of a large corporation once, I asked him if he believed that women had to work harder and be smarter than men to be successful in corporate America. He very honestly said, "Yes, they do. This isn't fair, but the situation is just what it is." As my mentor at TI told me, "The best way to be sure you get the job you want is to be sure there's no one else on the page with you." The higher up in a corporation you go, the more difficult this becomes.

WHO *REALLY* WANTS YOU TO SUCCEED?

It's crucial for a woman to know who is in her camp—which persons will defend her, promote her, and "die" for her. This applies to bosses and other superiors, as well as subordinates. Who wants her in their "foxhole"? Does she have a broad and deep network of relationships to protect and promote her? My situation at Texas Instruments is a good example of supportive mentorship. When I became the second female VP at Texas Instruments, I reported directly to two line managers, both male, rather than to the Corporate HR VP, Chuck Nielson, who was my mentor. That particular job was difficult because both of the line managers felt pressure to promote a woman VP—although both grudgingly agreed that "the company needs a woman at this level." I believe that the only reason I prevailed was Chuck's strong and open sponsorship. Everyone knew he was on my side and looking out for me. I had the comfort of knowing that no matter how difficult the line managers were to work for, I was protected. They knew it, too, and that helped level the playing field.

When I went to work for him, I was twenty-two and right out of college. Chuck was still young but older than I was—around 34. Chuck was certainly an excellent businessman, and he was confident enough to take on a young woman as his protégé. But there was an additional element that I haven't mentioned: he had started developing macular degeneration at around the time I was hired, and two years later he had gone totally blind. So he needed my help, and I needed his help. Chuck was and is a brilliant man, and the most determined person I've ever known. He not only wasn't going to let his blindness get in the way—he was going to succeed in everything he attempted. At the same time, he knew he couldn't achieve his goals alone. I was a workhorse and I did whatever he needed, whenever he needed it, and together we made it to the top of the corporation. This situation was good for him, it was good for me, and that's how long-term business relationships work. I had no doubts whatever that Chuck wanted me to succeed.

We should all be so lucky as to have someone like Chuck as a mentor! And not just a mentor in general, but a sponsor who will defend you, who will promote you, who will cover your back. Better than just one mentor is, in fact, a cluster of mentors who will teach you and support you. Everyone should have a number of mentors, a number of sponsors, and a network of relationships. Why a network? First of all, because people have different skills and knowledge bases. Second, people's career paths are unpredictable; people may be supportive of you, yet they may not necessarily be around for the long term. Third, you never know exactly how your relationship may develop. There may be ups and downs, differences of opinion, and political changes that can complicate the situation between you.

Should female executives focus on finding female mentors, or should they seek both female and male mentors? I believe the answer is obvious: both. You need to learn from everyone. At the end of the day, it's about everybody working together. And you can never have too many people in your camp. The more people in your camp, the less isolated you will feel—and, more important still, the less isolated you will *be*.

MORE BUSY = MORE ISOLATED

Women often believe that if you do good, good things will happen as a result of your efforts. To some degree, this is true. It's also true, however, that success requires other elements, and one of those elements is a web of supportive relationships. Many women don't understand that the higher they go in a corporation, the more the informal network of relationships is crucial for success. When they neglect relationships, they find themselves isolated from information and people that may be critical to their success. Yet women often neglect relationships because they are too busy doing "real work." The result is that women at the higher levels of management tend to have fewer relationships than is generally true for male executives, and thus there will be consequences of that isolation.

When women neglect these networks, they also may miss out on getting help with getting their work done. There may be other peers or other people who could partner with you to accomplish a goal. When you succeed, they succeed; you make sure they receive recognition for their input; and as a result of these interactions, a relationship is born.

Sometimes there's a tendency to work very hard and to be constantly busy to prove to yourself and to the people around you—that you're hard at work. The unfortunate truth, however, is that good work alone won't get you a successful outcome in upper management. It doesn't matter if you're the best at what you do. Excellence certainly helps, but excellence isn't enough. Why? Because almost by definition, corporate success means you're dependent on others, including people who know more about certain issues than you do. If you are a specialist in marketing and you become a division president, you may know a lot about marketing, but you probably don't know as much about finance, engineering, IT, and a host of other matters. By definition, you're going to have to depend on other people for their expertise. That's a very different situation from being recognized because of your excellence in a specific area of expertise.

There's another aspect to the situation. If you have neglected relationships and networks, then by the time you get to a higher level of management, you'll lack the resources you need. The situation holds true for men as well as for women. Anyone who doesn't develop his or her networks will be at a disadvantage. But it affects women more than men because women are more isolated from day one.

Liberty and Justice for Her?

TABOOS ARE ALIVE AND WELL

Taboos are another element giving rise to certain kinds of isolation. Consider these two issues: sex and attire.

Sex is definitely a minefield for women in the corporate field. There are probably two levels of reality in the C Suite. Most women know that any hanky-panky would be the kiss of death for their careers. Men, on the other hand, probably think that in theory, yes, it's the kiss of death, but in practice that isn't necessarily true. Some men gamble on dalliances. Some actually survive the consequences—at least as long as what has happened doesn't violate company policy. I know of a number of men who have married subordinates or even administrative assistants, but the consequences for women are almost always more severe. The bottom line is that any behavior perceived to be even the least bit flirty, suggestive, or inappropriate is a definite career-killer. This is true even if the behavior was misinterpreted or erroneous. Women need to be particularly sensitive to their behavior in settings where alcohol is present. There is simply a much narrower acceptable range of behavior for women. Any mistake in this area is one that the other people present may never forget.

Now consider the subject of attire. On the one hand, men have just two fundamental options: business attire or casual attire. Business attire generally means suit and tie. Casual means slacks and polo shirt or something similar. By contrast, women have far more options in terms of styles, fashions, and other "components" of attire. Especially in today's world of tighter and more suggestive clothing for women, respectable business choices are harder to find. Younger women who have only known tighter more suggestive clothing need to be especially sensitive to their attire around older men. In short, there are no "uniforms" for women analogous to those for men, so the choices are often difficult. A female executive can easily be accused of being suggestive, manipulative, too feminine, too revealing, or worse. On the other hand, if a businesswoman dresses in a way that's too conservative, she may find herself described as being drab, dowdy, or unisex. If she dresses in a way that's too fashionable or hip, she'll be criticized for drawing attention to herself. It's a no-win situation. Unlike attire for men, the model is much less clearly defined. We see comments about the hair, make-up, and dress of women in the news much more often than about their male counterparts. Just ask Sarah Palin, Nancy Pelosi, or Meg Whitman.

What are we talking about here? Basically, about double standards. Taboos are alive and well, but they often have more drastic consequences for women. This is an old, old story—and all the more depressing for being so old. But there it is.

Two other areas warrant mention: display of emotions and cursing. The corporate workplace has long accepted men's display of emotions including yelling, screaming, cursing, and the occasional throwing of objects. While responsible companies generally do not condone these types of behaviors, the male perpetrators frequently emerge from these episodes unpunished or with only a minor slap on the wrist. On the other hand, the acceptable range of emotions for women is much narrower and the consequences much more severe and longer lasting. The ultimate taboo is still crying. Tears still convey a sense of weakness and fragility in the workplace. In fact, they may be triggered by rage or deep anger and have nothing whatsoever to do with weakness. Regardless, tears at work, particularly in the presence of a male boss or peers are absolutely unacceptable and deadly to a woman's career.

By now you may be thinking, "Oh my goodness. In the face of so many factors that isolate women and make their career goals and ambitions so difficult to achieve, is there any hope? Where do I begin?!"

Have faith, ladies. Knowledge is power. Now that you understand some of the challenges for women in corporate America, you can fill your toolkit and be sure you're doing everything possible be the successful woman you desire to be.

CHAPTER 4

TAKING CONTROL of YOUR HOME and YOUR CAREER

I want to start this chapter a little differently from the several that have preceded. Specifically, I'd like to step back and consider our topic—how women can advance their careers in top management—and I'd like to view the issues through a slightly wider-angle lens.

It's true that our topic focuses chiefly on women's careers. However, women don't advance their careers in a vacuum. All of us have to consider the work issues we face in the context of our personal lives. And for all women, the issues we face regarding home and family are paramount. For this reason, I'll explore these issues throughout this chapter by considering how the "home front" influences us as female executives.

Liberty and Justice for Her?

THE STRUGGLE FOR BALANCE, AUTONOMY, AND EQUALITY

For years, all of us have been hearing about how women struggle to achieve work/home balance. I'm sure there will be no end to this discussion! What interests me at the moment is how the phrase "achieving balance" is usually used to refer to a cluster of *time* issues. How does a woman get everything done?! How does she find enough hours in the day to pursue her career and simultaneously attend to her family's needs? I want to consider a different aspect of balance: the balance of power and influence within a marriage. In all marriages, there are gradual changes over time in how the spouses divvy up power and decision-making. Sometimes these changes go well; sometimes the process of change becomes problematic—often in ways that work against the wife's wellbeing, both in the short and longer terms.

By way of example, let me tell you about Laura. For many years, I had been hearing about her difficult marriage—and through all that time, she was unable to change the dynamics with her husband. I had tended to assume that her complaints were simply a way of blowing off steam. Then, to my surprise, I learned that her marriage really had fallen apart. Laura filed for divorce.

What I didn't know about the marriage, however, was that Laura's husband had never fully backed her professional aspirations, nor had he ever shared with her much of the decision-making about money. She had to "ask" to spend anything he earned. She was "allowed" to spend her earnings on items, but as he earned significantly more money than she did, he held the purse strings very tightly. He had used the power of his earnings in different ways throughout the marriage—and he now aggressively pursued every post-divorce financial advantage. Laura was left high and dry. The shame, anger, and humiliation she felt over this situation are simply heartbreaking. Her ex is a successful doctor who pulls in a very high income, while Laura's career never advanced much beyond the middle ranks of a not-for-profit foundation. She makes only a limited income. Is this set of circumstances her husband's fault? Well . . . partly. But the difficult truth is that Laura never really stood up for herself or acted to fulfill her dreams. She let things drift with her husband, and she never made any plans or took any steps to ensure her financial wellbeing in the event that the marriage faltered. The outcome? A very strong woman who had great potential was devalued in her marriage and never seemed quite able to ignite her career. What hurt her the most, however, was her husband's indifference to her throughout their marriage. She felt she never received any support, much less recognition, for her life. And she never took a stand to advance herself. This lack of agency has left her stressed both emotionally and financially. She's going to have a tough road ahead. Most troubling is her struggle to take control of her life under what are now very difficult circumstances.

Perhaps you'll say, Well, of *course* she'll have trouble! She's a member of a generation in which women have often relied on their husbands for everything, especially money, and who don't stand up for themselves. No wonder she's in a bind: she never really took control of her own destiny. Women of later generations wouldn't fall into this trap.

I wish that were true! Unfortunately, the sad reality is that many bright, strong women of every age—even women who are happily married—can end up losing track of their goals and ambitions much too easily. Here's an example of a younger person in a happier marriage that is still a potentially risky situation.

Liberty and Justice for Her?

A friend's daughter is 31 years old. Adele is an engineering MBA who made around $200,000 a year. When she and her husband decided to have children, Adele took several years off from work. The planned three years became five, then seven, and now eight so far. She has just recently given birth to her third child. The oldest is eight years old. And during this time of childbearing and early parenthood, Adele hasn't worked in her former area of expertise. I asked my friend about her daughter, and the reply concerned me. "Oh," my friend said, "I don't even think she's worried about that." I found this response disconcerting, to say the least. I said, "If she isn't thinking about it, she at least ought to *start*—and the sooner, the better." The good news for her is that a technical career may be easier to reenter than some others.

I know very little about what Adele and her husband have discussed. What I fear is that she doesn't yet realize what she has relinquished. If that's the case, this is an unfortunate situation. She isn't taking into account all the issues that a couple will face. Frankly, I hear about this type of abdication far too often. For instance, many couples don't plan in advance whether the wife should work during her pregnancy—or how long she should stay home after the delivery. This approach is a roll of the dice. Maybe she'll be lucky and avoid feeling sick in the morning or sleepy in the afternoon, but I suspect she'll have to cope with some of those symptoms. Maybe her boss will cut her some slack because she's pregnant, but maybe not. Following the birth, she'll need to take at least six to eight weeks off just to recover physically—not to mention what will happen if she continues breastfeeding. If she goes back to work while still nursing, she'll encounter all sorts of complicating factors in the workplace. And from there on out, she'll be a mother confronting yet more challenges.

Why are these issues so disruptive? It's not just because of the short-term challenges, which are significant and often intense. The problem is that precisely at this point in a young woman's career and life, so many expectations will weigh on her that she may simply fold her tent, bury her childhood and college ambitions, and focus on mere survival. This phase of life is also a critical time in the marriage. Every young woman should be insisting and ensuring at this time that *she* gets the help and support she needs. But given the expectations of women and mothers in America, this may not happen. As we now know, women are subtly channeled from early in life to be the caretakers of everyone else in their life, and often at the expense of their own career development and personal satisfaction. If the most positive reinforcement they ever receive is for these other-focused attitudes and behaviors, it's no wonder that ambitions go by the wayside. Similarly, it's no surprise that they continue to behave so "selflessly"—this is the only behavior for which they get positive reinforcement.

So am I suggesting that Adele *shouldn't* be both a mother and a high-performing career woman? Not at all. What I'm saying is that she—and all smart, capable, ambitious women—should take stock of these issues early and plan ahead. It's true that all of us have to improvise to some degree, especially since so many aspects of family life are inherently unpredictable. But "just winging it" isn't adequate preparation. Young women must learn that true equality and autonomy in a marriage and in family life are possible. Just like men, women should be able to expect and nurture an independent self-image.

A New Model in the Home

I'd be the first person to say that women face major challenges in balancing work life and home life. However, I'm deeply concerned that so many otherwise strong, bright women—women who look ahead and plan for the future in so many other ways—just cross their fingers and hope for the best when assessing their careers. Too many women tend to assume that if they just work hard and "do good work," everything else will fall in place.

I know all too well that there are no easy answers. I certainly don't claim to provide any panaceas. Rather, my goal in this chapter is to nudge all women who aspire to upper management positions to strive for financial and emotional independence and equality in their home first and foremost. The key here is early awareness. If a woman waits until her mid-30's or later to reach this insight, she may have much more difficulty maneuvering in the world of work, and it may also be more difficult to change behaviors later in her marriage. Without fully understanding the need for her own financial stability and autonomy, women may tend to be more cautious and less confident as they nurture their careers and home life. Being in control of one's life brings confidence and a sense of ownership. Young women, especially, may tend to be more uncertain than men are about her leadership role in her marriage. Traditionally, a man's first and most important goal is to provide for his family. A man can actually provide for his family by being more successful in his career. A woman, by comparison, must "provide" for her husband, her children, perhaps her extended family, and finally for herself. If there is time and energy left over, then she can think about her career. The unspoken expectation is often that the husband will be the primary breadwinner; and if this is the assumption, the breadwinner role may also carry with it a disproportionate share of the family's power, influence, and leadership.

In response to this traditional "default" approach to the spouses' career development, women need to take a much harder look at the situation. Even though she may not be the primary breadwinner, each woman should ask herself these questions: Does she have an equal say in how money is spent? Who controls the checkbook? How does the couple make financial decisions? If a young woman isn't careful, she may find it all too easy to just let her husband "take care of everything." One reason to plan is simply the reality that in the United States, more than 50% of marriages currently end in divorce. While it's always tempting to see your own relationship as safe from this fate, ignoring the risks may put your career—as well as your family's stability—in jeopardy.

Balancing home and career is probably the hardest challenge for any woman to master. I know this all too well—I struggled with these same issues myself for many years! But until recently, most people believed that the challenge was about time management. We now understand that the issue of balance is also about power, influence, decision-making, and leadership in the family. The vow "to obey" no longer belongs in a wedding ceremony.

Why is it so difficult for women to take hold of these issues proactively? Anna Fels (quoted earlier in this book) very articulately asserts that traditional assumptions regard the heart of femininity as *giving*. If a woman isn't careful, she will relinquish her autonomy and her sense of agency. Here are some of the reasons I see for this situation:

Reason #1: Women Don't Plan for an Independent Life within Marriage

Being married or having a partner does *not* mean a woman shouldn't continue to have control of her own life. Men who are fathers generally don't face anything like hurdles routinely present for mothers who work in the business world. In any case, women tend to simply plow ahead. Men do the same. But the difference is still that women tend to take care of themselves *after* they have met the multiple obligations toward home and extended family. She should ask herself if her spouse or partner carries the same level and scope of responsibility within the family. Just being the primary breadwinner doesn't absolve either spouse of other responsibilities. But we're all so busy on a day-to-day basis that we just try to get through the week, through the month, and through the year. There's rarely an opportunity for a woman to stand back and ask, "What do I want to do?" or for a couple to ask, "What do we want to accomplish together?" Most people—especially during difficult economic times—have their hands full simply surviving. Planning for an equitable relationship may seem like the least important thing to do.

I remember many, many times during my careers when a woman I knew would go on maternity leave, and the question among her colleagues would always arise: "Do you think she'll come back?" As a mother, you really can't answer that question until you've had the baby and have started to explore whether or not you'll stay home or, alternatively, you'll arrange childcare and return to work. There will be a million issues going through your mind as you make those decisions. I've observed a fair number of women over the years who didn't come back to work after the six to eight weeks of maternity leave. Others returned to work, but only after a year or two—or three, four, or five. Of women executives overall, relatively few I've known had children; and of those, more have had non-linear career paths.

When I've looked at the bigger picture that's evident in news reports, it's clear that some high-achieving women have chosen not even to marry at all. Each woman has her own reasons, of course, for marrying or not marrying; but in some instances, the decision to remain single apparently stems at least partly from women's concerns that conflicting obligations will damage their careers. Again, this is a personal choice. But it's troubling to me that women should have to face either/or decisions of this sort—a situation that is surely more common for women than is true for men.

Reason #2: Personas May Be Out of Sync

Each of us has multiple personas—our roles and the "faces" we present to the world as a daughter, as a mother, as a sister, as a wife, as a member of a work community, and so forth. This multiplicity of these roles is part of what can make life so rich. A problem that many of us confront, however, arises when there's a large gap between our persona at work and our persona at home. The integration of these different personas into a sense of wholeness is critical for a woman's being able to develop a strong sense of agency. The more different each person's personas, the more challenging the integration can be.

In any marriage, the roles ebb and flow. What I've seen most often in executive women is that they are either childless or they have what is generally referred to as a "trailing spouse." (I'm not crazy about the term, but that's what it is.)

What often becomes stressful and frustrating is when the persona is out of sync with the financial reality or with the social roles. Part of the dilemma is this: when a woman has a really strong position at work, and when she may be in a support-only position in her marriage, how does she cope with dissonance if the two roles aren't in sync? When I found myself in social situations where spouses of work peers and bosses were present, I always felt uncomfortable. Often I was the only woman in a work group, with the awkward result that in social settings, I never knew whether to converse with the women (who were the spouses of my peers) or with the men themselves. Likewise, my husband wasn't "one of the guys," but he generally didn't want to hang out with the women. We usually just struggled through an evening or weekend. I still believe that these conflicting roles act to make women feel isolated: you are neither fish nor fowl.

Reason #3: The Husband's Mixed Messages

Another challenge occurs if her husband "talks the talk" but doesn't "walk the walk." I've known some couples in which the husband *seems* to be committed to equal careers, but in reality he is less than supportive of his wife, and he favors his own career. He feels that his work, his role, his future must come first. He isn't sufficiently supportive of his wife's aspirations. This invariably puts the wife in a bind as she tries to advance in each of her several roles. While men's roles may also vary in different settings, here again he isn't necessarily expected to take care of everyone else's needs first. He is first and foremost expected to provide for his family. A woman often feels "selfish" if she pushes for her career when her husband is "sacrificing" to provide for her. There may be less-than-subtle pressure on her from many fronts to "support her family"—which in reality means *consistently* putting herself and her own needs last.

Reason #4: Breaking the Mold

As we noted in Chapter 1, a lot of behaviors are culturally determined. I believe that men don't set out to be selfish; however, I do believe that our culture makes it much easier for men to act in their own self-interest than is true for women. There's still a general assumption in many marriages that men's schedules are more important, or at least should come first, and should include more discretionary time. A husband may consider it just a given that he'll go have drinks with the guys after work, or that he's free to get together with work associates for golf on Saturday. It may be much harder for his wife to take time for herself. During my careers,

I took little or no time for myself! I'll have more to say about this issue later in this chapter.

The reason that these attitudes flourish is the sense of male entitlement that our culture allows and even encourages. As women, we often enable this entitlement by picking up whatever ends up undone. Life runs on men's schedules. A man may in fact be quite devoted to his family, yet he may not necessarily track what his wife needs. It's not ill intentioned—it's just *entitled*. Women may complicate their own situations by picking up the slack and enabling such behavior. You just keep working and never stop to question why. Habits developed early in a marriage may be hard to break later on. A smart young woman is constantly aware of her role in the marriage. Is it what she expected? Is it what she wants? Does she have as much control over her destiny as her spouse does? What are the most important currencies in her marriage—and how are they divided?

Reason #5: There Are Few Models for Women

It can be frustrating and discouraging to see how few role models women have in upper management. This is especially true because the successful businesswoman has a more complex career path compared to her male counterparts. Men often manage to have fairly linear careers. The main reason is simple: their careers aren't disrupted by the huge biological and personal event of pregnancy. They may share in the child-rearing duties, but they don't spend nine months pregnant and then have to cope with early phases of childcare, such as nursing, that only women can do. Most highly successful women either just work themselves to death fulfilling the multiplicity of roles demanded of them, or else they have non-traditional, non-linear career paths. A few have spouses who have accepted roles not as the primary breadwinner. Women at high levels of the corporate world may be single, divorced, or married but without children. There's more variety for women in terms of personal circumstances of these sorts than seems true for men. In my experience, it's rare to encounter a male CEO who doesn't have a fairly traditional family. His wife may work, but her work role is often subordinate to the husband's career. The very fact that a woman may be the primary breadwinner and that her husband has primary responsibility for the family makes that family "nontraditional." There simply is no clear model for women in high-level careers.

These are the elements that often determine the timing and development of a woman's career. It's the most difficult issue to solve from an employment standpoint. There certainly are issues as well for women who don't have children, but there are significantly fewer, I believe, than for women with children. This situation creates a very loaded set of complex decisions for women.

A TALE OF TWO EQUALITIES

From the standpoint of equality for women, the circumstances may (perhaps ironically) have progressed further and faster in the corporate world than in the domestic realm. Why? Because in the business world, there's at least some agreement on what equality looks like, and there are structures and procedures in place to foster it. In the domestic sphere, by contrast, there are few givens. There are no set standards. What goes on between a man and a woman or between two domestic partners is a most personal and private matter. This is exactly how it ought to be. However, the outcomes of this personal, private approach aren't necessarily clear-cut or without internal conflicts. Roles and activities are often culturally and personally determined, and cultural expectations and personal aspirations may generate conflict. Dilemmas may result in family expectations when personal goals are contradictory.

To complicate matters, the roles for men are often more similar throughout the culture than are the roles for women. What do I mean by this statement? Simply that a group of men probably has a more similar pattern of activities at home and at work, generally speaking, than will be true for group of women.

Here's a further and slightly more radical thought. It's possible that at the moment, women have achieved a degree of safety in numbers throughout the workplace. If a boss or a company is discriminatory, women have recourse through grievance procedures and even class-action lawsuits. By contrast, one wife coping with one husband in one marriage has fewer resources at her disposal. She can't exactly participate in a class-action lawsuit against her husband! Even in a marriage where the spouses have a fairly even division of labor, they will have family issues and cultural assumptions to cope with. In addition, early in the marriage, as a couple establishes the rules for its household, one spouse or the other will generally take a stronger leadership role while the other person may assume a subordinate role in the division of duties. In our culture, it's often still assumed that the husband will have more of a leadership role. That's not always the case, but there's certainly a predominant pattern along these lines, especially for men at the highest levels of our corporations. Which spouse makes more money? Out of necessity, the stronger role is generally assigned to the person who provides the greater share of family income. Even in marriages with a high degree of equality, sheer financial necessity will drive a lot of decisions. The situation is understandable: if a couple puts their well-being in jeopardy by insisting on equality at all costs—even if the equality leads to a significant shortfall in income—that decision may lead to problems. (It's true, however, that sometimes a woman's income may increase faster in later life as some of her other obligations diminish.)

THE MOST CRITICAL FACTOR: AGENCY

All of the issues we've discussed so far have led me to conclude that whatever else, a woman must have a strong sense of agency. (The standard dictionary definitions of *agency* include "the capacity, condition, or state of acting or of exerting power" and "the fundamental desire to have control over one's own life.") She needs to control her own life and then gain a sense of accomplishment and pride so that she is responsible for her own actions. So far, so good. Many women do. But what about women who don't have a strong sense of agency? How do they acquire that?

The first step is awareness—awareness that it's acceptable to want your own goals, your own plans for reaching those goals, and your own sense of achievement. Unfortunately, there are many women—mothers, especially, but plenty of others as well—who equate ambition and personal goals with being selfish. They worry that they're self-centered. They fear that if they have their own goals, and especially if they strive to attain those goals, they're shortchanging their children, spouse, or others. Even taking this first step toward awareness can be a real struggle.

I know all about it—I've had to walk this path myself for a long time. I'd like to tell you a little more about my story because I think it clarifies some of the issues.

Starting Early

It may surprise some readers to hear me say this, but one of the first people to foster my sense of agency as a woman was my father. Dad was adamant about letting me make my own decisions. He advocated the same thing for my brothers as well. Believe me, not all of my decisions were good! But as long as they didn't cause any major harm, my father and my mother let my brothers and me make our own choices—and then experience the consequences. My father not only *allowed* this approach, he *insisted* on it. My mother tells the story that when I was in third grade, Dad told her to quit fixing my hair for me: "She's ten years old—old enough to do that for herself. Stop doing it for her." Mother was aghast. Apparently I looked horrible for an entire year. But this situation was about far more than just hair care. I learned to take care of myself—and not just my hair. If that's the environment in which you grow up, you do things differently than if other people are constantly intervening for you. And I think the fact that I was not pampered but, rather, was treated just like my brothers set the stage for how I've interacted with men throughout the rest of my life. I was never expected to defer to my father or brothers, everybody played by the same rules. This exercise in self-empowerment strengthened me. When I turned 16, I had to get a summer job—even though dad was a doctor and I didn't have to go to work for financial reasons. That's simply what we did in my family. As a young adult, I found that my independence was paying off. One reason for Chuck Nielson's decision to hire me at Texas Instruments, as he told me later, was that I had backpacked all over Europe for three months—not something that a lot of twenty-year-old women did at that time.

However, this early experience of gaining agency wasn't the whole story. I started full-time work at 22. Fortunately, I gained entry into a good company and I felt that I wanted to stay. But after the first three or four years, I began to get a sense of what it took to be successful. There weren't very many other women around. By then I had married Larry, my high school sweetheart, and we were settling into married life. I knew that having a child wasn't ideal at the time. TI professionals worked every Saturday at that time, so I couldn't begin to imagine how I'd manage both a family and a career. As a result, I just kept putting off the decision to start a family. I knew that the juggling act would be difficult anyway, and I worried that parenthood would cause the wrong kind of attention at work. There were just going to be too many hurdles in the road as it was.

Finally, after seven years, Larry got persistent about parenthood—to the point that I remember one discussion in which he said that he didn't understand why I didn't want kids. He thought I should go talk to our minister about it. I couldn't really articulate my fears yet. Perhaps my concern was that if I'd said, "Well, I don't know how I can continue to work and also have a family," Larry would have said, "Don't worry—you won't have to work." That wouldn't have been a good answer to me. On the contrary: giving up my career was a frightening prospect. So, frankly, I just put off the decision. I was late in having children—or at least "late" for that era. (I was 29 and 31 when my kids were born. Back in the 70s, that was considered late.)

Over the next several years, following the births of our daughters and during the early stages of parenthood, I didn't have a moment to myself. Larry was a great father, but he was extremely busy with his growing law practice, and he also took some time off occasionally to hang out with his pals. My recollection is that I was the psychological parent. Larry did other family tasks, certainly. But he managed to take time for himself; generally speaking, I didn't. The reason I didn't was simply that a massive amount of work at home always had to get done. Mind you, we had a full-time nanny, and both of us had our parents nearby in Lubbock, and they were wonderful about helping us out. In spite of all of these resources, this phase proved to be a difficult, busy time. We both had very demanding jobs. The reality was that Larry's willingness to take time for himself, and my inability to do so, caused me to resent him from time to time. It never occurred to me simply to do it.

From his standpoint, I had time to myself on business trips, and those occurred more frequently for me than for him. He would take care of the kids at those times. He knew that my business trips weren't just for fun, but he felt that they allowed me time away, and it's true that the evenings could be relaxing. Yes, I was away from the kids overnight some of the time. And, yes, I would go out and have dinner with colleagues, which could be enjoyable. Travel is often cracked up to be something great and wonderful . . . but after you've done it long enough, it's hardly R&R. Maybe you like the people you're with; maybe you don't. So, yes, I had this kind of time to myself. But I didn't see that in the same light as going to have drinks with the guys, or going off on a golf trip. It was very difficult.

What does my history say about agency? First of all, the insights I reached occurred through the evolution of my thinking, not all at once. Second, developing agency required me to go out on a limb. Third, I waited a very long time, which made it all the more difficult when I finally demanded a change. We reached a point where Larry wasn't willing to make a move for my career. He believed that our financial situation should be the primary driver of what we did for the family. I agreed that this was important, but in fact, we both had well-paying jobs. He made approximately double the income that I did, it's true, but it's also true that I wasn't going to make more money unless I took some of the bigger jobs available. I recall my boss telling me when a VP job came up at TI: "You can say no if you want, but you won't be asked forever." He was trying to be careful. He understood why I wasn't taking the jobs. I don't know how else to put it, but something just broke when all of that happened. I had to make a decision that I was either going to be in charge of my life and have a full say in my marriage with Larry—or I wasn't. All I felt at the time was anger, frustration, and helplessness. I don't know if that was good or bad, but I had to be willing to risk my marriage for us to move forward. So my solution to that was just to take the job, figuring that we would let the chips fall where they may.

To Larry's credit, he didn't respond to this news by saying, "Okay, this is broken—we're done." We just plodded through. Larry tried to find a job in Austin, but he couldn't find one that appealed to him. In the meantime, I was already working in Austin. We could only afford one house, so we sold the house in Lubbock and bought a house in Austin. We also bought a townhouse in Lubbock for Larry.

Somehow we made it work. But for a while, we didn't know the outcome. If Larry hadn't been willing to see this period in our lives through, this situation could have gone sour fast. I probably would have divorced Larry—if he didn't divorce me first! It wasn't just the importance of the job itself that mattered to me; it was *the importance of being able to do what I wanted to do*. It was much more about the autonomy/agency issue than with anything to do with the job itself. The job was great—I was the second female VP at TI, and all that. But what mattered most was having the freedom to discover what I could do. I finally felt in control, even through taking this step was difficult and frightening.

But shocking news came a year later. TI went through a major restructuring, and they wanted me to work in Dallas. Larry got pretty angry over that. And rightly so: if he had given up that great law practice and senior partnership to moved to Austin, it would have been a bad situation. So I moved myself and our kids back to Lubbock, took the job in Dallas, and commuted to Dallas from Lubbock *every day,* four days a week, for four years. During those years, Larry and I worked through the disagreements between us. Larry was much more supportive once I was doing the Dallas commute. At the end of four years of commuting, however, I recognized things weren't going to get any better. I was exhausted by the travel. Larry was still making more money than I was. So I made the decision to leave TI and to see what was around the next curve. But once again, what I feel is critical here is that my decision to leave was mine and mine alone.

One of the things that Larry said to me at that time was: "If you want to quit, that's fine. But this is absolutely, completely your decision. If you're not happy with how it works out, don't blame it on me. This is *your* decision." I think these remarks are a credit to where our relationship was at that time. His words were an honest statement and one that was important to bring to the forefront. He probably worried that I would blame him—that I'd say he was the reason for my decision. He wanted no part of that.

If I were going to insist on agency, then I needed to take full responsibility for it. And I did. In addition to thriving in my several positions at TI, another deep satisfaction came from seeing how my relationship with Larry actually deepened and grew as a result of the choices we made together. Even though I loved Texas Instruments, it was time for me to move on.

WHAT I'VE LEARNED ABOUT BALANCE

To conclude our discussion, I want to offer my distillation of experiences about balance and how it affects women's lives—including the lives of executive women.

My most important realization is that women must strive for equity and balance in all aspects of life. If you don't, you won't have equity and balance in any of them. It's just too difficult to try to live multiple, non-integrated roles. In addition, there are no reasons--other than those we create for ourselves—for a man and woman *not* to have a union in which both spouses share equitably every element of their life together. Both their roles may ebb and flow as circumstances change, but total equality for women in all facets of life is surely within reach. We only need to grasp for and acquire what is rightfully ours.

In addition, I want to offer these further thoughts to ponder.

Discuss These Issues Openly with Your Spouse

Here are the most critical questions that a husband and wife should raise, discuss, and explore together:

- Who makes the decisions—and *how* are they made?
- Are these decisions truly equ*itab*le?
- Whose career takes precedence?
- What is the power structure within a family?
- Does the person who makes the most money set down the rules or guidelines?
- Are decisions always based on finances?
- How is the money spent?

The goal in exploring these issues is to help your spouse support you and your career as fully as his own. By implication, the husband or partner needs to be as fully supportive of his wife and her career aspirations—as supportive of her career as she is of his. Doing so means accepting balance in the home regarding child care, domestic duties, and the "second shift" overall.

Have a Plan and Aim High—You Can Always Change Your Specific Goals

Women should assess what they need for their own financial independence if there are changes in the marriage or family situation overall. Essentially, this means following the old adage: "Hope for the best; prepare for the worst." The emotional side of the situation is that to be an equal partner, a woman needs to be equal both professionally and financially. As noted earlier, a woman needs to cultivate her own sense of agency. Agency is what motivates us to take initiative, to achieve, and to be self-sufficient. A woman cannot have agency if she abdicates her autonomy on her wedding day. Agency is associated with individual achievement and the exercise of power. Even if spouses decide that the woman will remain at home, there should still be the same respect and financial stability between *both* parties.

Understand the Nature of Work in Top Management

Women assume that the higher up you go, the harder you have to work. They may define "harder" as a greater quantity of work or as meaning more difficult work. The assumption is that going up the ladder two or three or four more steps may mean two or three or four more times the work. But that's not necessarily true. Why, then, do we make this assumption? I think part of it is that women equate the amount and quality of their work with their success. The truth is that the higher up you go, the more you have to depend on other people and on your ability to get other people to work with you. If you're doing that, I believe that you can manage the situation well. You've only got 24 hours in a day, so what do you do with that time? What are your priorities? How do you manage yourself? I think the situation is more about women not clearly understanding what it takes to be a successful leader.

This is a double-edged sword. The whole time that I was in general management, I was literally on call 24 hours a day. This is just the nature of the role. However, I think it's a myth that the higher up you go, the less free time you have. You may need to be accessible 24/7, but you can still say, "I'm leaving early this afternoon, because I want to take my daughter to a medical appointment."

NO MORE WONDER WOMEN!

People these days often joke (though the "joke" isn't very funny!) that to manage her home and business life, a woman today has to be a Wonder Woman. All too true! Young women, especially, are vulnerable to this pressure. Why? Because they don't discover until their mid-twenties the realities of our long-held cultural ideas about femininity, childrearing, and organization within a home. Older women (like me) also face challenges when we finally do "get it" and try to make changes in our marriages and work life. But the most inspiring and rewarding reason for throwing off the Wonder Woman delusion is the new level of trust, commitment, and mutual respect that a husband and wife can discover in a truly equitable relationship. Perhaps that is what a "perfect mate" is all about.

No longer do you always need to put everyone else's needs ahead of your own—and then, continuing to be all things to all people, throw on your Wonder Woman outfit and head for the office.

CHAPTER 5

DURABLE RELATIONSHIPS AND NETWORKS—AND HOW TO BUILD AND USE THEM

Several times throughout this book I've mentioned Jill, my boss at Cox Communications, and I'm going to talk about her at other times, too, simply because I learned so much from her about what women can become in the corporate world. I want to talk about her again now—this time regarding the importance of networking for female executives.

My relationship with Jill was full of surprises. First of all, I had never been exposed to a strong, positive corporate figure who happened to be a woman. I had certainly never worked for a woman before. I remember talking to Jill about this not long after I'd started working for her, and I remember telling her that it felt different to work for a woman. She asked me how. "I don't know that I can put it into words," I replied. "I think there's just a familiarity, a trust.

It doesn't mean that I think you give me extra breaks—or that I would expect you to—but I feel comfortable in the relationship. I guess that's the best way to put it." Another thing about Jill is that she is so obviously authentic. She enjoys being a woman, and she values her femininity. She is also direct, strong, bold, and brave. She is transparent and sometimes vulnerable. I believe that she has taken the best of traditionally feminine traits and masculine traits, and she has melded them into her own unique leadership style. The result is strength of character combined with resolve that attracts people to work for her.

But our one-to-one relationship, though powerfully inclusive, was just the start of what Jill taught me. There were also specific, deeply important ways that Jill showed me what women could do for one another—what we could *be* for one another—in corporate settings. Jill worked hard to make the other female executives at Cox comfortable with and supportive of one another. She wanted us to develop a network among the women that the men already seemed to have developed. It wasn't that the men had intentionally excluded the women; rather, they had simply established a network based on their own camaraderie and common interests. Until that point in my career, I'd worked in settings where nothing similar had happened for the women. First of all, I'd never been around enough women execs for a network even to be possible; at Cox, however, there were finally enough of us present—something like 30 percent of executives. But even then, I just don't think it had ever occurred to some of the women to start networking in the manner that Jill taught us.

I remember the first time Jill showed us her style of networking: an evening get-together for a number of women who worked for her. I felt as if we were almost doing something wrong. It wasn't as if we got together and gossiped about the guys. We talked about our divisions, our projects, and whatever other aspects of our work came up. What mattered was the cohesiveness and the support for one another within the group that Jill was developing. I don't even know if she was fully aware of it. During the course of that first evening, one of the women said, "Jill, what would you say to the guys if they did something like this?" I remember her answer clearly: "Haven't you ever been to a golf course?"

A NETWORK OF HER OWN

One of the crucial missing pieces of the puzzle I'm describing throughout this book—how to advance female executives' careers—is this: understanding the importance of relationships and networks. By this I mean long-term professional relationships with women and men alike; business and organizational networks; and mentors, associations, and other interactions that can foster and enrich a woman's career. All of these relationships and networks are crucial to any executive's long-term success. I should note, however, that I regard the importance of woman-to-woman relationships and networks as especially crucial for female executives. Just as the British author Virginia Woolf stated that every woman should have "a room of her own" in which to foster her own creativity, I strongly believe that every female executive should have a female network of her own.

To explore this topic, I started this chapter with a story about Jill because she was such an extraordinary mentor. She taught me so much about so many things that it's not surprising that she taught me much of what I know about networks. For this reason, I want to revisit some of the other ways that Jill enriched my professional life and boosted my career.

The first time I went to a managers' meeting with Jill as my boss, for instance, we had some free time between the end of the day and the evening activities. She looked at a couple of her female general managers and said, "I've got to run over to the department store. You guys want to come?" All of us said yes. A male manager might have said, "We're going to go to the bar. Care to join us?" He certainly wouldn't have suggested a shopping trip! Jill was probably being somewhat exclusive in her invitation, but, interestingly enough, one of the men present said, "I like to shop, too—can I come along?" Jill invited him to come along with us. So three of us women and the guy went shopping. It was just the most amazing thing. I'd never seen anything like that happen in a business setting. We shopped, we looked at stuff, we laughed, and we acted like a bunch of girls on a shopping trip—but we also included the guy, who was trying to find a gift for his wife.

What this incident did for me was, number one, to bring me closer to the other women, who I didn't know well yet. It also brought me closer to the male exec, who was also relatively new to this management level. In short, it was the beginning of a particular relationship with everyone who went on that little excursion. We didn't talk about anything really important. It was just the proximity and the acceptance—knowledge meant that, yeah, we were all part of the group. It was just different. It was a particularly woman-friendly occasion. To be honest, it was also kind of a shocker to me, but it was so welcome! In a strange way, that event really gave me a boost of confidence about being at Cox and about starting to understand how things were going to work there. It was totally energizing. Jill's actions in spontaneously setting up this event seemed a natural extension of her personality—both as someone who was an excellent leader in general, but also as someone who fostered change and growth among her female peers and subordinates. And, too, as someone who was authentic.

A second example occurred when Jill had scheduled a business meeting in my city. Since she was the guest, we went out to dinner that night. Her leadership team consisted of one woman and three men that she brought with her. That night, she and I had a long discussion about family. I've never gone socializing with business associates and experienced a situation where the evening chat focused on family issues. Throughout the evening, I kept noting to myself, Hmmm, this is different! Jill was every bit the boss, but the tone was different—not necessarily better than in the past, but different and infinitely more "woman-friendly."

Here's a third example. At one point, Jill had an opening for a division president. Five or six of us who were already division presidents reported to her. Jill had at least three women division presidents at the time. Now she asked me who I thought might be a good candidate for the open post. I recall saying, "Well, whatever else, you can't add another woman." She just about went ballistic: "I can't believe that you of all people would say that! Why the hell can't I?" She was so right. I ended up laughing at my own remark. I told her, "You know, you're just going to have to be patient with me."

WHY NETWORKS ARE SO IMPORTANT

Organizations are communities. Whom you know, what you share with the people you know, and who shares with you—all of these elements are crucial. Information, knowledge, and understanding are the currency in any organization. If you only do your job, you'll miss out on the opportunity to buy and sell things important to your career. It's critical that women understand this point as early as possible in their careers.

But there's an ironic aspect of what I'm describing. Generally speaking, women are highly effective at communicating (i.e., thoughtful listening and nuanced talking) with one another in personal relationships. We put a lot of time, energy, and effort into all kinds of interactions with female friends and relatives. Yet the communications in business settings are different. Women haven't necessarily excelled in this regard—and in fact, it wouldn't be way off base to say that we tend to be deficient in this area. Why? Well, I have some theories. Managing relationships in a business environment does, in fact, use some of the same skills as those employed in friendships; however, the tasks are very different in some respects. My opinion is that many women in business miss a lot of opportunities—especially opportunities for connecting with other women. Networks are about much more than just talking to other people. Good communication skills are just one dimension of successful networking.

To understand the situation more clearly, we need to return for a moment to the distinctions we've made between *leadership* and *management*. Women are often perceived as being very good managers. But management is a set of tasks in which you're dealing with the *formal* channels of communication, the *formal* structures of the organization, and the *formal* aspects of the business that are fully documented and available to everyone involved. Remember, leadership is the art that takes over where the science of management ends. As you go higher in an organization, there's more art involved and less science. The rules are less well defined—or perhaps not defined at all. Leadership focuses as much on the intangibles of how you accomplish things as on the formal, documented processes and procedures of running the business.

A New Paradigm for Ambitious Women

What Are the Implications?

First and foremost, we need to realize that when we're talking about relationships, networks, and other aspects of upper management, we're really talking about power and influence. It's certainly true that women are gaining power and influence in the business world. But traditionally, men have wielded power in ways that women haven't. Men at the higher levels of an organization are more comfortable with the notion of wielding power and with understanding that doing so will have significant effects on their ability to get their job done. This level of comfort has probably allowed men to shift more easily from management skills to leadership skills as they climb the corporate ladder.

Second, there's the issue of linear versus nonlinear career paths. When a man goes to work in a corporation or some other organization, he generally has an understanding that he'll have a linear path in his work life. This understanding isn't a "given" for women. For this reason, it's not surprising that the group in power—generally speaking, men—will tend to view up-and-coming bright, young men as the likeliest candidates for inclusion. This won't necessarily be the case for bright, young women nearly to the same extent as for their male counterparts. The situation I'm describing means that senior male executives may not be "tracking" women's careers as closely as they tracked young men's. They won't be including as many women as men in their networks. And in turn, the situation means that women need to communicate effectively, energetically, and creatively to make themselves visible—visible both to male peers and senior managers, and also (perhaps especially!) to other women.

Third, it's worth noting that in the upper levels of management, there are still far more men present than women. In some ways, this situation bears a resemblance to other venues in which men have excelled, such as in the field of sports. The notion of a corporate team isn't so dissimilar from a collegiate team or even a high school team, groups in which men often already feel at ease both regarding notions of leadership and teamwork. As a result, many men are already comfortable with sharing power and with wielding power by the time they get into upper management positions. This situation spills over to notions of inclusion. If you're already part of a group, and if you are included to the fullest degree, then you have more flexibility to move around within that sphere. If you're not as fully included, what you do isn't as fully trusted, recognized, or rewarded. Here again, women tend to be left on the sidelines in one sense or another, and we need to work harder and more imaginatively to make sure we're included. It's true that women today have more opportunities to participate in sports and other team-oriented venues, but they don't have nearly as many as men do.

By comparison, what happens when women reach upper management? First, we find ourselves in the minority. Second, we may find that the kinds of friendship and the kinds of relationships that we've cultivated throughout childhood, adolescence, and early adulthood are significantly different from the *kinds* of relationships that are necessary in a business setting. Personal relationships among women often stress openness, reciprocity, and shared feelings and vulnerability. In addition, these relationships are frequently about giving. Personal relationships are just that—personal. By contrast, business relationships focus heavily on trading information and favors that result in influence, power, and hard-nosed credibility. Business relationships are much more object- and action-oriented.

A New Paradigm for Ambitious Women

Because There Are So *Few* of Us…

What I'm describing here provides a start in understanding the importance of networks in the day-to-day lives, as well as the long-term careers, of every woman in upper management.

First, precisely because the numbers of women decrease significantly as you work your way up the corporate ladder, there's a heightened need for women to support one another. When I use the word "support," I don't mean to imply that you'll agree with everything your female colleagues say or do. I don't mean that you and the other women will even like one another. What I mean is that it's crucial for women to listen, provide feedback, reach out, and make a special effort to offer one another mutual support precisely *because there are so few of us present.* You may engage with another woman on some particular subject or project; and, if there turn out to be issues that you can't support, you'll be able to back away. But saying that women need to support one another means—just as it means regarding men—that you'll still need to be selective and thoughtful; however, you certainly need to reach out to women because so few men (or significantly fewer men, anyway) will do so.

Second, keep in mind some of the gender-related aspects of this situation. Let me pose it as a couple of questions: Are women more supportive of other women than men are in practical ways? And are women more likely to be strong allies? Not necessarily. However, there may be a familiarity among women that you'll share because you're a woman, too. Men have a similar familiarity with one another. So, if you're reaching out to other women, and if all other things are equal, then those relationships may be among the strongest and most special you establish. For me, Jill at Cox Communications was a great example. Other women were supportive peers or superiors as well. Relationships of these sorts can be especially strong. Traditionally,

107

women have ignored or else haven't cultivated woman-to-woman business relationships because, frankly, they're more focused on the men. There are more men than women present in upper management. They have more power. Women executives' focus on male powerbrokers is understandable. However, I believe that as women, we tend to overlook the possibility for power and influence among ourselves. Fostering mutually supportive relationships with other women certainly doesn't mean that you can't develop strong, creative relationships with men. And you should.

YOU CAN *NEVER* START TOO SOON

What we've discussed so far now brings us to the point of taking action. And action is crucial. While the informal networks may *seem* to be less critical for younger managers, the foundation for long-term relationships, networks, and trust start forming the day you start work. If you don't build the relationship and network résumé with all the care and diligence of your job history, your career will never really take off. An accountant is highly unlikely to get an accounting job without the proper credentials. Likewise, as you reach the upper levels of any corporation, your networks and relationships are often as important as your job history. What's interesting, however, is that this fact often isn't acknowledged or discussed. Everyone just "knows" who is in your camp. But if you have no camp, you'll miss the whole show.

Here's the crucial question: Who's got your back? If you wait until you need a network, you're sunk. It's absolutely critical to know who will defend you when you need the support, as well as who will promote you when opportunities arise. More importantly, who will *make* opportunities for you?

A New Paradigm for Ambitious Women

Here's a cautionary tale to illustrate this situation. Shortly after I started working at one corporation, I needed to hire a VP of Finance. The second-in-command to the previous VP was a woman. Her resume was good, and she had seventeen solid years of experience. However, the rest of the leadership team was lukewarm about endorsing her for the promotion. When I spoke with her previous boss (the former VP), he carefully avoided a strong push for promoting her. I told her the truth following this conversation: "You are qualified for the job on paper, but you don't have the support of your proposed peers, nor of your former boss." She was both surprised and hurt. I wondered why she had so little idea about their opinion of her.

So sad! Here's a woman who was competent . . . but who hadn't bothered to build networks—*any* networks—and who now discovered that no one would support her. She was a very strong second-in-command. She was a real workhorse. She was highly competent. I'm sure she made her boss look very good. But aside from her competence and her strong work habits, her overall image was deficient. She didn't come across as particularly professional in how she projected herself. She was a little too laid back. I didn't see her demonstrate a lot of leadership skills. But where I think she really lost the game was that as she came up through the ranks over the years, she had never asked—and no one was ever straight with her—about her real strengths and weaknesses. Let's face it, competence and knowledge are just the baseline. Everyone has to have those attributes. Had she ever asked her boss, "Would you support me for this position if you were to leave?" No. She had just assumed that she would be the best choice simply because she was next in line. She didn't have strong relationships. She just provided information to the people who were one level above her—those who would have been her peers. There was no one in her camp when her moment of truth arrived . . . and she didn't even know it.

Meanwhile, her potential peers didn't see her as one of them. My take on her was that she sat in her office and ginned out the numbers, she attended an occasional meeting, and she issued her reports, but that was all she did. There was nothing wrong in terms of her competence. But now the question arose: should I select her? Because I was new to this company, I toyed with the possibility of overlooking the issue of leadership because she had the knowledge—and I really, desperately needed her knowledge. But because I was so new to the company, I knew I had to learn the politics. I was fearful she couldn't help me because she wasn't a "player." I thought, "She'll get killed in meetings because she isn't a player, and she won't be able to be my eyes and ears about things I need to know. I don't know enough yet to help her and get the information I need, so this isn't going to work."

The shocker to me was that when I told her directly that I had these reservations—speaking in a diplomatic way—she went straight to her former boss, and he phoned me right away to read me the riot act: "Why did you tell her that?"

"I told her because *you* didn't," I responded.

He didn't understand the situation at all. His silence—and his unwillingness to be honest with her, which might have prompted her to take steps to be less isolated—hadn't helped her at all.

In a later conversation, however, I told her, "If you stay in my organization in your current position and help me, I'll help you become eligible—or else I'll tell you why this situation is never going to work. Either way, I'll be straight with you."

Her response: she became angry with me because I hadn't put her in the job.

Soon after that, she followed her former boss over to another division. She trusted him more than she trusted me. What's interesting, though, is that since then, she has come up to me on each of several occasions when I've seen her—even within the last year—and she has told me, "I've always appreciated what you told me back then. You were the only person who was ever honest." However, she was afraid to make the switch to someone who was really willing to support her.

SOMETIMES "GLUE," SOMETIMES "GREASE"

In today's fast-paced and competitive environment, networks sometimes work better than the more formal organizational charts and communication vehicles. They can "grease the skids" and make difficult circumstances easier to navigate. They can also be the "glue" that holds relationships and interactions together.

When I was at Cox Communications, for instance, I almost never went to a budget meeting or other important meeting without knowing ahead of time what the likely outcome would be. I did this by talking to peers who had knowledge of the subject and were willing to share information. I did it by having an informal "meeting before the meeting" with my boss to be sure that we were on the same page and that neither one of us was going to experience any surprises in the meeting. And I enlisted my direct reports to talk to their contacts about potential questions or barriers we might encounter. We all know that the formal relationships diagrammed in organizational charts are important. You can't ignore them; you can make them work for you. But in a sense, networks and informal relationships are the white space on the org charts. They are also the foundation for the trust that must exist above all else at the highest levels. If you ignore this "white space," you do so at your peril. Horizontal interactions take place through networks rather than through hierarchies.

The higher you go, the more networking matters: it's the very basis for communication. Men have known this for a long, long time. Now women need to learn it and practice it.

I believe that both the formal and the informal channels are necessary. You can't run a company without any formal channels; those have to be present to get the work product out the door. Particularly at the lower levels, almost the whole focus is about getting the work done through task orientation, and it's clear that you need these formal structures. The higher up you go, the more the focus is about direction and decision-making than about work processes. In short, you need *both* the formal and the informal systems. Among the companies I've worked for, the Cox model was the most impressive. My team would frequently discuss issues among themselves before a meeting. Almost always, some number of my direct reports would get together before the formal meeting and have time to talk about how they wanted to see the meeting take shape. Occasionally, I'd throw a curve and take it off in a different direction. But I was trying to be sensitive to the time and effort they put into the issue before the formal discussion—at least they'd get a fair hearing about some of their thoughts. My job was to provide the leadership, but also to provide a fair hearing for all good ideas and comments. On rare occasions, I'd just have to call time out. I'd say, "Okay, we have differing opinions, so I'll make the call on this one. We're going to do X and not Y." But what enabled me to make the best decision was the informal interactions that went on first.

Here's the budget process as an example.

In the cable business, the budgeting process is the single biggest formal task that we had to do. It was always a massive effort. We worked on it for several months. We would go to Atlanta and essentially present our business plan for the next year. Sometimes we would also do also a three-to-five-year, long-term plan. But certainly the very specific plan for the next year would end up being a contract between my senior executives and myself about what I would deliver for the following year. During those couple of months, while my team and I were putting together that budget and the presentation, there would be many calls and discussions either between my boss and myself, or, for example, with the corporate vice president of marketing, all to make sure that we're on the same page. By the time we got to our budget meeting, we had pretty much resolved any major problems to the best of our knowledge.

What I appreciated about Cox was the spirit of cooperation. I never, ever doubted that my bosses wanted me and my team to succeed. Those informal channels were critically important. And I think Cox was most conducive to those sorts of relationships being developed and maintained. In other corporations, the situation was different. There wasn't nearly the acceptance of give-and-take before meetings. There was a more competitive edge to meetings.

The environment in some companies will prompt you to keep your head low and do the best you can—a far cry from the open, informative approach I experienced at Cox. Sometimes people hoard information and tell others things that aren't completely accurate. Why? Just to throw you off. While it is wonderful to have an open, inclusive, proactive culture like the one at Cox—one in which you don't have the kind of an environment I just described—your network is even more important. It's true that strong, honest relationships may be hard to find, but they will be even more important for your survival and success.

NOT WHERE YOU GO FOR COMFORT AND PERSONAL INTIMACY!

Where does this leave us? Relationships and networks are crucial. The time you put into them will pay off in ways that are intangible but invaluable and absolutely necessary. I want to make a few further remarks, however, about how they work and what they mean.

First of all, I believe that business relationships are just that: business relationships. Even among women who are your associates, they are your associates, not your girlfriends. If you must unload something of a personal nature, or if you need a shoulder or personal confidante, do *not* burden your business associates. Your image as an executive is vitally important. The person you share personal information with today may be your boss or competitor next week. Be a savvy woman. Always remember that every conversation can potentially be a job interview. Divulging too much personal data may make you seem weak or needy.

Sometimes women—and men, too, for that matter—may be looking for friendships in the business world. It's not that you can't find friends in that setting, but you have to be really careful. I'll be blunt: you're probably better off focusing on your business activities and on your business relationships. I recommend that you step carefully—or step smartly, at least. Friendships aren't the same as networks. After a period of time, you may develop some off-line friendships, or something like friendships, with men and women you work with, but you have to be careful. You really can't cross over the line of just telling someone everything unless you're in a crisis mode. Even then, I still think you should keep your private life out of your workplace.

The key is to be discreet and *always* to remember that you're in a business environment. During the workday, it's easy to do that. After-work gatherings, however, can get a little bit looser. Alcohol can become a problem. Particularly for women, social situations can become risky, even devastating. Women simply have less room to maneuver, behaviorally speaking. A man can get drunk and act like a jerk, and people will generally say, "Oh, he just had a bit too much to drink." If a woman gets tipsy, says something impulsive, or behaves in a way that she normally wouldn't have, she may never be able to get the situation out of the company's collective memory. She'll have less flexibility and forgiveness about stepping outside normal positive behavior. Later, when senior executives are considering two people for a job, even the smallest incident in her group's social memory may become a problem. People may say, "She's really good, but . . . Well, I'm just not quite sure about her."

In short, you have to be very careful. That's one of the advantages of having networks with women: you can maneuver a little more in those groups. At some of Jill Campbell's meetings, for instance, someone might refer to a personal event, such as the death of a relative, and get emotionally upset—but that expression of emotion generally wouldn't cause any problem. None of us would have given it even a single thought—other than perhaps to comfort her and then move on. I will say that even with other women, emotional behavior cannot become the norm. However, if she had gotten emotional in a mixed group, or in a heavily male group—the situation would've been different. When a decision has to be made about her, that memory of her emotional expressiveness would be still be vivid. Because jobs are so competitive, a minor incident like that might be the one thing that causes the decision-maker to say, "You know, I think we should go with him instead of her. I just feel better about him."

Men may not even be aware that they're making a judgment of that sort at the time. Yet when push comes to shove—when there's a question of whom to select for a job, who's the go-to guy, or who's the strongest person on the team—you want someone who is a superman or superwoman. You can't be seen as presenting any problems. In that sense, you have to protect that persona. You always have to remember that you're in a business setting. During my first year at TI, my boss, Chuck Nielson, told me, "If I ever even hear a rumor about you, you are in trouble." This was tough but also wonderful advice—truly great advice. It may not have been fair, but it was honest and realistic. It helped me because it warned me in advance what I'd be facing.

But here's the downside. All of these issues may cramp a woman's ability to be authentic. If you're constantly having to be more circumspect than your male counterparts, people sense that; so, in a sense, you're damned if you do and damned if you don't.

The truth of the matter is that there are business associates with whom you can be more fully yourself. There are others with whom you can't. You'd better be right about who falls into each of these categories.

RELATIONSHIPS AS CURRENCY

Networks are reciprocal by nature. To some extent, networking is a form of barter. What you exchange is as real a currency as money. For this reason, you have to cultivate who is in your network, and you need to be careful about favors asked and received. Networks essentially allow the transfer of energy. Like any energy, you have to monitor intake and outflow. But what I'm describing is a legitimate exchange process: relationships are channels for the exchange of energy.

A New Paradigm for Ambitious Women

Here's a story about this kind of "currency" between two women.

I was still at Cox when I received a very thoughtful note from someone named Kathy. She had participated in the Betsey Magness Leadership Institute program at some point in the recent past, and she was writing now to welcome me in advance for my being accepted into that same program. I read her note and thought, "Oh, that's nice—I don't even know her, yet she still wrote to welcome me." Two years later, when I was working for Time Warner, I was one of four division presidents. The four of us reported to an executive vice president. One of the division presidents had just left after being promoted. So now there was an opening, and my new boss, someone I didn't know very well, but whom I liked a lot—Wayne—said, "Connie, I'm considering a lady in South Carolina by the name of Kathy." When he stated her full name, it rang a bell, but I couldn't recall from where. In any case, Kathy came in for an interview; she and I talked; and we hit it off. I finally connected her with the earlier note. There was a business connection, and I had great respect and appreciation for what she'd done for me earlier. Wayne asked my opinion of her, and I said, "I think she'd be a great choice." And he hired her. It was amazing, the difference I felt in his meetings after that—because now, half of us were female division presidents. It was just an incredible shift of power and influence. And of course this turn of events had come about at least partly because of our earlier connection. I probably would have endorsed her even if she hadn't reached out to me so much earlier, but her doing so certainly cemented my regard for her.

Part of what made the difference was just the familiarity of another woman. In fact, I would venture to say that this issue was a great part of it. There was just a sense of *balance*. I suspect that if you asked both of us, we'd say that the other's presence made each of us a little more confident. It wasn't that we necessarily agreed with each other all the time. As a matter of fact, I was probably closer in philosophy to one of the men than I was to her. But it still made a difference to have another woman present. All of us have had experiences of being in the minority, whether in terms of nationality, ethnicity, or something else. And I think there's a way that each of us will relax when, even if you're still in the minority, there's someone else, or several people, present who are more like you.

Another issue is that if you're in a small minority within a group—whether in terms of gender, race, nationality or some other factor—there's a risk of being stereotyped when you speak up. People may say, "That must be the women's opinion (since she's the only woman present)." You tend to be seen as the spokesperson for the group you're coming from. This perceptual bias can be very subtle. I don't believe that in a corporate world today, people are intentionally dismissive. But you may worry about that issue, which in turn may prompt you to be more hesitant to speak your mind. By contrast, if you're one of 50% of the women present at a board meeting and you speak up, you're seen as more of an individual: "That's Connie's opinion"—rather than, "That's the female perspective."

There's a lot to be said for balance and familiarity. You can have familiarity with men in a business setting—and I mean familiarity in a positive way. I've had as close relationships with a few men that I've worked with over the years—or even closer relationships—as what I've had with some women. So it's not impossible. But the relationships are different. In a perfect world (or in the perfect company), both men and women have long–term, positive, mutually beneficial relations with other men and women. It's a win-win for both, and the company enjoys the benefit of the diverse, best performance of all.

A New Paradigm for Ambitious Women

AMONG YOUR MOST CRITICAL RESPONSIBILITIES

How do all of these discussions add up? I realize that we've covered a lot of topics—many aspects of a complex issue. But here's what I believe is the crucial take-away in this chapter.

Most companies don't document or communicate the need for networks and relationships. If they do, it comes under "teaming" or "ability to work well with others" or other inauspicious headings. Companies should be much more forthcoming about the power and place of networks and relationships, and they should acknowledge the reality of informal, undocumented structures. Unfortunately, they don't, as it's difficult to document and describe and almost impossible to "measure." Men do well at passing it along to their friends and associates, while women often aren't "insiders" of such networks and do *not* utilize other women nearly enough. For these reasons, women need to fill the gap on their own. It's crucial for you to grasp the need simply to know that you need to do it. You need awareness. You need to forge your own relationships and networks.

Here are some specific things you need to do.

Don't Isolate Yourself

First, get out of the office. Even if you're the only woman in the group, leave your office and drop in someone else's. There will be plenty of pretexts. You can ask about a project, or you can pick some other issue—but in any case, get out of your office and move around. Drop in on your peers. It may be up to you to start the ball rolling. It's much easier to ask someone for something if you have already established a pattern of communication. I have found that women ignore their peers more than they ignore their subordinates or bosses. This can be a big mistake.

Arrive Early, Leave Late

Second, go to meetings early. More women than men tend to arrive right at the starting point. Why? Because they've been working and they don't want to "waste time." Well, that fifteen minutes before the meeting isn't a waste of time. Anything but! Information is being shared there. Personal connections are being strengthened. You don't have to show up early at every single meeting, but you should certainly show up at some. Also, don't race out the door the minute the meeting ends, either. Hang around for a minute, see what's going on, and see if there's anything worthwhile to stick around for. I can't tell you how many times I've had staff meetings when, at lunch time, the guys would all go off to a restaurant—but the two or three women present would leave to go run errands. Invariably that would happen. Just think of the opportunities they'd miss!

When I interviewed a male friend who was the division president in another division, we were talking about whom he supported among the women, and he told me about a particular vice president. I asked him about the issue of lunch. "Does she go out to lunch with you?" I asked.

"No," he replied.

"Who do you go to lunch with?"

"Generally with X, Y, and Z." He listed three of the guys by name.

"Do you think that ever makes her feel left out?"

He thought for a moment and then said, "You know, it probably does. But what you're saying just never crossed my mind." He thanked me and said, "I should have been more aware of that."

True! On the other hand, she could have taken the initiative herself, too, and she could have made herself present when he got ready to go to lunch. She could have made herself more available as part of the network.

All of these approaches build relationships. Equally important, there are kinds of "soft data" that you acquire at a meeting—or before or after the meeting, for that matter. The soft data may be a matter of learning who seems to have an alliance with whom, what the mood is regarding a certain issue (perhaps at variance with official opinions or with the hard numbers), and so forth. But many times it's much more of a social issue. Here's an example. With my leadership team, they reached a point where they could routinely manage themselves quite well. They would wrestle with an issue among themselves before they brought it to me, which was appropriate and wonderful. I always had to keep an eye on it because I had a couple of really strong personalities who might wear down or even steamroll everyone else. And I had to be careful that certain issues got fully aired. But overall there was a dynamic of what got said at the meeting, what got said before the meeting, and maybe what got said after the meeting. There were other times when we would agree that something was going on that needed to be done in a particular way, and two or three of my folks would get together and decide to do it somewhat differently. As long as the job got done, I didn't care. But if the woman who wants to go higher in the organization isn't part of that group, she's really out in the cold.

Toot Your Own Horn

Very often women are way too modest about their accomplishments. We just don't like to advertise what we've done. You have to be careful how you do it, but make sure that your boss knows it. In subtle ways, you need to let others know what you've done, too. Be sure to toot your own horn often enough—and loud enough. I think also that men and women need to be conscious of what they can do to help their peers. Sometimes it's information, sometimes it's just a pep talk: "Hey, that was a tough meeting, but you handled yourself really well. If you need help on the numbers, I can get you those." Be sensitive for opportunities where you can help someone, but also be smart about who you're helping, because, to be very candid, you don't want to champion someone who's wrong.

IT'S ALL ABOUT TRUST

Trust is unconditional. You either trust other individuals or you don't, and vice-versa. Is there a perception that this man or this woman knows the right thing to do and has the character to do it? The higher up you go, the more the choices generally aren't black-and-white. Sometimes they're "worse or worser," or good or better. Does the person have the competence, the character, and credibility to get the job done? At the highest levels, you get things done through *people.*

I want to close with a final story about Jill. By 2005 I had been working for her about five years. During a ski vacation in Colorado, I heard three separate rumors that Cox was considering a sale of some of its divisions. When I heard the rumor for the third time, it concerned me so much that I called Jill from my hotel. "This is probably just a stupid rumor," I said, "but I want to hear you tell me so. That way I can enjoy my time here."

She went completely silent. At that moment I knew that this wasn't a rumor after all. She told me, "I can't believe you heard this. I'm so sorry you had to hear it in this manner."

Then I was the one who gasped. We talked about the situation.

After a while she asked me, "You think I should call and tell Janet?"

Janet was my peer in another division. "Absolutely," I said. Then I added, "Jill, you and I both know that a secret isn't a secret anymore when two people know about it. I'm not upset—I'm just glad I know, and by all means you should call Janet."

Which she did. So there was a level of trust there. I wasn't upset that she hadn't told me yet. There's a time and a place for this sort of thing. I trusted her enough to know that she had done what she was supposed to. I also wanted my peer, Janet, to know. The three of us worked for the next year on that sale. It was one of the most difficult times of my life. I didn't know it at the time, but this time was also the greatest learning opportunity I was ever to have. The ease with which Jill, Janet, and I worked together was amazing. We often disagreed, but the trust was solid. The sale was a success. I will always have a special place in my heart for those two women . . . and to this day I would do anything possible to help them in any way.

CHAPTER 6

IT'S DIFFERENT AT THE TOP

I want to challenge some standard assumptions about what women encounter at the upper reaches of the corporate world. Many executives assume that the abilities and actions that have gotten them to a middle level in a corporation will take them to the top. All they have to do is work a little harder, a little smarter, or a little longer. This is not the case. In fact, the rules, structure, and networks change significantly at the highest levels of an organization. The nature of what you do at those levels is fundamentally different from what you do in a mid-level position. For this reason, your approach to gaining access to the top—and your approach to thriving if and when you get there—needs to be much different from what most people assume. Ignoring this reality may greatly limit your chances of climbing higher.

MANAGEMENT AND LEADERSHIP ARE DIFFERENT

Here's a reality that women executives need to accept: there are two career ladders, not just one. The first is the management ladder; the second is the leadership ladder. As Colin Powell has noted, *management* is a science. Specifically, it's the science of getting work done through more formal standard operating procedures, rules, and communication channels. By contrast, *leadership* is the art that takes over where the science of management ends. Leadership is about the ability to go farther than anyone thought possible. Leadership is about navigating through uncharted territory in a way that helps people accomplish things they didn't know they could accomplish. Leadership is about getting things done through people. I believe that women tend to rely more on management skills, while men often seem more comfortable in their use of leadership skills. Why? I believe it's because women tend to be more isolated by their sparse representation in the C Suite compared to men. In fact, women are just as capable at leadership as men. There's no reason that women can't be effective, creative leaders. However, many women need to become much more aware of everything that's going on around them and how they relate to people, events, circumstances, and opportunities. Women also need to take charge of their careers in a positive, proactive manner. In short, they must develop a sense of *agency* early in life. Agency will foster both management and leadership expertise.

There are a variety of leadership styles and techniques. A Catalyst study shows that the best leaders aren't necessarily the best known or the most flamboyant. The Jack Welch types of leaders may be impressive, but they don't necessarily leave behind a legacy that can be sustained when they depart from their posts. The leaders who deliver the longest-term, most sustainable results are often more humble and less flamboyant (though equally strong and confident). We just don't hear about them as often. The characteristics of leaders who are both successful *and* enduring are more than just the so-called "strong, rugged, individualism" that gets more media attention. These more humble leaders are also likely to be strong and rugged and confident, but they express those characteristics in different ways. For instance, one of the most interesting approaches I've learned about has become known as "servant leadership." This philosophy and practice of leadership, first proposed and defined by Robert Greenleaf, urges leaders to achieve results for their organizations by giving priority attention to the needs of their colleagues and those they serve. Servant-leaders are often seen as humble but strong stewards of their organizations' human, financial, and physical resources. They are no less committed, relentless, or resilient, but they demonstrate those leadership traits in different ways.

Let's talk in a little more detail about management and leadership. If you're in a management position—certainly when you're in the middle levels of management, and perhaps at somewhat higher levels as well—you manage or run an area of functional expertise. That area may be finance, engineering, information technology, human resources, or something else. If you're at the top of that function in the organization, you generally have a deep and strong knowledge of that area of expertise. Your expertise is, in fact, what got you that job.

But when you reach senior leadership levels in a corporation, you make a leap from managing the function in which you're an expert to managing multiple functions. You may be an expert in one or maybe two of those functions, and you may have greater or lesser knowledge of the others. But by definition, the skills and the knowledge that got you into upper management are now only a part of what will make you successful from that point forward. The nature of the job has changed—and your skill set needs to change, too.

What are the implications? Virtually no one—or at least no one I've ever met—is an expert in all of the different disciplines at the top of a corporation. Even if an executive possessed such diverse expertise, she wouldn't have the time to go and literally manage each one of the areas. For this reason, leadership becomes critical. As a senior leader, your job isn't to be the resident expert in any one specialty. Your job is to take what is generally a complex team and, first of all, to articulate your direction clearly; and second, to ensure all of these various components work together to achieve the goal. Finally, your job is to check often to make sure tasks are on schedule and achieved effectively. As President Reagan famously said: "Trust—but verify."

What I'm describing here essentially reveals the difference between management and leadership. In leadership, there are certainly many remnants of management present. You continue to hold regular meetings, such as those necessary for setting a budget. You continue to ensure that the formal communication and work processes are operating as they should. You also work hard to have the best people in the most critical jobs. But the core of your fundamental task is more evident on the leadership side. By definition, you are now heavily dependent on everyone underneath you to do their jobs, and to do them well. You rely more on the support roles that your peers, your boss, and your direct reports play to assist you in their various corporate functions. All of a sudden, this aspect of scope of responsibility becomes critically important. Why? Because very few senior executives ever complete all these tasks entirely on their own. You can't be an island. You need other people's help.

There are specific skills necessary for this kind of leadership. According to the Center for Creative Leadership, the skills most central to successful leadership are: being resourceful, doing whatever it takes to reach your goals, being a quick learner, being decisive, and leading employees. If you possess all of these skills, and if you apply them well, you probably stand a good chance of success. It's not just that you're managing more generally; you are also relying on a big-picture capacity as a leader, as opposed to the more laser-like focus on specific tasks as a manager. You're fostering the synergy between all these different systems and departments under your guidance. You have become a generalist. It's worthwhile to note, however, that being a generalist is only part of your role. The real role of a leader is to understand where the organization needs to go. To have a plan for getting there, you'll undoubtedly have lots of people helping you, but you *own* that plan. Ultimately, if the plan fails, you own the failure. It isn't the failure of the people under you. If people under you are failing, it is your job to replace them or to take whatever steps are necessary to help them succeed.

Here's a story about my own experiences when I found myself rather unexpectedly shifting from management to leadership.

I started at Cox Communications in 1997. My area of expertise at that time was Human Resources. When I was promoted to VP and General Manager and became responsible for the P&L of a business unit, my job changed completely. I simply got thrown into the deep end of the pool. I could no longer depend on my good work in HR alone; I was now responsible for Finance, Engineering, IT, Marketing and Sales, and several other functions—all functions where I had little or no expertise. Frankly, I was scared to death that first year, and I probably had good reason to be scared. The situation was very tough and very tense. However, I felt confident that my boss, Jill, believed in me, and I had great trust and confidence in her. However, the situation was mine to make or break. I don't think I assumed that she was more likely to help me just because I'm a woman. Also, I was so new to Cox that I didn't even know there was a strong culture there—a culture fundamentally receptive to and supportive of female executives. But in an odd way, my uncertainty actually helped me. As much as anything, it demanded that I realize that I had to take responsibility for my performance and myself. Cox offered me an opportunity to find my personal agency and to discover my true strength. However, it required that I do things I had never done before and to trust in myself.

It required me to take on a job where my personal expertise suddenly wasn't the primary criterion for success. I reached an abrupt insight that I needed to rely on a different skill set. It was the age-old sink-or-swim situation: I was either going to figure this out . . . or I wasn't. Jill put the situation bluntly: "If you don't dramatically improve these numbers, Connie, you'll leave me no choice." The picture got very clear very fast! I didn't resent her bluntness or her priorities. Jill had no choice—she simply couldn't have a unit leader who was not performing. That's one of the rules at the top. But for me, what was most important is that I had finally accepted the mantle of leadership—and the ownership that comes with it. I had to take complete responsibility for my success or failure—and to do so for probably the first time in my life. I have been fortunate enough to have had a great mentor at TI; and in that earlier position, it had been safe to learn and grow. But I had always been in a support position. Now I faced one of the critical challenges of leadership: you have to be bold and fearless. Being fearless doesn't mean that you throw caution to the wind. Rather, it means that you accept this premise: you owe it to your people and your company not to allow fear to cripple you or otherwise inhibit you. You use fear to be ever diligent and to sharpen your vision. Now I understood. Being bold is having the confidence and vision to take aggressive but smart risks. And now I had to make the leap in order to advance. I call it a leap of faith, because that's what it is. It was one of the most energizing, exciting, and wonderful times of my life. Once you move from fear and uncertainty to boldness and confidence, you lose the numbing fear of failure. It becomes unimportant. All you care about is doing the best you can, and being secure in the knowledge that you will find the best path.

WHAT YOU CAN DO

I have no doubt that you and every other woman will need to make your own leap at whatever point you arrive at a similar point in your executive career. But is the willingness to make that leap your only preparation for shifting from a management point of view to a leadership mindset? No, of course not. There are other ways—crucial ways—by which you can prepare yourself. Fortunately, there are significant steps you can take to acquire the leadership skills you'll need in the upper realms of corporate life.

For me, the most powerful influence was the Betsy Magness Leadership Institute. This organization absolutely opened my eyes to personal possibilities I had never before considered. But I had to be immersed in a group like that for extended periods of time over a span of many months to really grasp the issues clearly. My boss, Jill, directed me to apply for the program. I didn't want to go. I had been through numerous leadership programs, and had been in Human Resources for 20 years. I felt the only thing I *didn't* need was leadership training! And I knew I had a lot of knowledge about leadership skills and traits. Why, then, should I spend weeks and weeks over a period of eighteen months to learn more about leadership. Well, I still didn't "get it." I didn't know what I didn't know. I didn't know that I didn't have the confidence, daring, and courage that I truly needed. As it turned out, I found those things as a result of my experience at the Betsy Magness Leadership Institute. That group changed my behavior—and my life.

In addition, my various mentors over the years—especially Chuck Nielsen and Jill herself—taught me about many aspects of leadership that benefited me immeasurably. I have also gained much knowledge by reading books about leadership—both classics and more recent publications—over the years. (See Appendix 2, Further Reading, at the end of this book for suggestions.)

Here's a summary of my thinking about the most important attributes of leadership that ambitious women executives need to develop.

Attribute #1: Personal Agency

As I mentioned in Chapter 5, standard dictionary definitions of *agency* include "the capacity, condition, or state of acting or of exerting power" and "the fundamental desire to have control over one's own life." Agency is fundamentally a sense of self-confidence that results in taking action to control one's life. It propels us to navigate a course through life even as we encounter challenges and obstacles. People with a sense of agency are more likely to be assertive, to accept the responsibility of power, and to make thoughtful, resolute decisions. I can't imagine a successful executive who doesn't possess a high degree of agency. I believe it's particularly important for women to develop their sense of agency early in life, preferably in childhood. A woman will live her adult life differently if she has always been independent and has "owned" her own actions and decisions.

Attribute #2: A Sense of Connection

Women—and men, too, but perhaps women especially—need to have a connection to other people. Women have a need to connect, and that's a skill or trait that they can translate into the corporate arena. Connection includes the benefits of what you gain from other people but also the benefits you can provide to others. Connection potentially revives nurturance to all parties involved. In a corporate setting, connection allows a sense of context and common endeavor. My work at Texas instruments, Cox Communications, and Time Warner helped me learn the importance of communicating with and supporting other women. Over time, I understood that "connecting" in the business world has different attributes than connecting in a more personal sense. During my time at the Betsy Magness Leadership Institute, for instance, there was a two-hour meet-and-greet occasion on the very first day. All of the participants were sitting at five tables—five or six to a table—and each woman took a turn getting up, introducing herself, and making some comments. We were supposed to comment about our expectations for the program. At least half of the women present made some reference to feeling reluctant about participating: "I'm not really big into women's clubs," or "I'm not much of a joiner," or "My biggest fear here is that this will become a bitch session."

Then, as the program took shape, we learned how to network in the true sense of the word. It was amazing that most of us didn't know how to do that already. Many of us were great communicators, but we didn't understand the difference between (on the one hand) communication and networking, and (on the other hand) building enduring relationships. More amazing still was that *we didn't know what we didn't know.* True business networking was just nonexistent to many of us, so we didn't miss it precisely because we didn't know what it could be. We didn't even know how to look for it. It wasn't in our scope of awareness.

Attribute #3: Keeping It All Together

Women often struggle to unite all of their many roles, activities, and responsibilities. This struggle takes place on a personal level but also on a professional level. A goal that all of us strive for is achieving a sense of personal integration so that our lives feel whole. When attained, the resulting sense of personal integration has benefits for every aspect of our lives—including our abilities as leaders. This is an issue that women more than men may struggle with, since women more often pay equal attention to their home life as well as to their professional roles. Personally, I think this issue is where many woman executives feel stymied. If they can't integrate their home life with their work life, it becomes an energy-sapper as opposed to an energizer. If a spouse isn't supportive of a woman's career—and willing to share home tasks equally—a woman may feel overwhelmed by the sheer volume of demands on her time and energy. But more importantly, if a woman's life partner doesn't truly value her ambitions and goals as much as he values his own, a divisive home environment can develop. Or, more likely, a woman may simply subordinate her own life to her husband and family. One result is that leadership skills—and the individual leader's overall confidence—may suffer.

Attribute #4: Understanding Yourself

It's probably true that just as we can never fully understand other people, we can never fully understand ourselves. The human mind is capable of filtering, distorting, and even blocking perceptions and insights about our own thoughts and feelings. Complete clarity about our own emotions, motivations, and intentions is probably impossible.

However, attaining a degree of relative personal clarity is possible and desirable. As a woman performing each of your many roles, you're far better off if you can see yourself and your actions clearly. You'll see yourself in perspective. You'll understand yourself better in the context of your family, your community, and your work environment. As a leader, too, you'll make better and more insightful decisions. While wholeness is always a goal, it's important to have clarity of vision if and when that goal falls short. We all know that life is a series of twists and turns, so the more we can step back from the individual moments and assess what is happening, the more likely it is that we can make sound decisions regarding our actions and decisions.

Attribute #5: Being You

I consider being authentic to be a fundamental prerequisite to being a leader. This dimension is so critical to trust and credibility! If you can't be yourself—if you're constantly trying to be someone else—you're always going to be less than the best you can be. If you don't know yourself, how can anyone else know you? If people can't know you, trust and credibility will never happen. As women, however, all of us are under constant, almost unrelenting pressure to be someone other than who we truly are. I don't need to elaborate on this point. But this pressure is profoundly damaging to our sense of authenticity. This situation has terrible consequences for women executives. For this reason, being authentic is both one of the hardest tasks we face and one of the most remarkable achievements when we can attain it. The minute you negate yourself or try to be someone else, you lose your authenticity, which means that you damage your credibility, which in turn essentially stops your career advancement.

It's important to note that these factors may change over the course of a woman's career. For instance, personal agency may look different at each of several stages. In the earliest stage, agency will generally focus on learning skills and becoming aware of institutional circumstances. A woman will gain skills in her field and will widen the scope of her confidence. Later, she may focus on the ability to accomplish significant tasks and to figure out the best ways to shoulder the responsibilities. Later still, she may recognize that her field may or may not provide the long-term outcomes that she desires, so agency may require taking steps to change course. The malleable nature of these issues can be a major challenge for many women. However, the changes throughout a career aren't sufficient reason to avoid the challenge. On the contrary, if women can have opportunities to be exposed to some of these issues earlier rather than later, they can prepare themselves better for the inevitability and opportunity of change.

RISK TAKING, POWER, AND INFLUENCE

All serious executives must be adept at taking risks and at using power and influence. What I always try to remember about courage and risk-taking is this: courage isn't the absence of fear; rather, *it's the judgment that someone or something else is more important than the fear.* Fear and anxiety are natural emotions for a new leader to feel. They can sharpen your vision and raise your energy level. The more you focus on the job and spend your energies in a positive constructive way, the more the fear diminishes. This diminishment of fear then becomes a habit. One of the most important aspects of power and influence is using them wisely and not using them in an abusive manner.

Your "fear threshold" helps you make thoughtful decisions rather than fear-based decisions, which in turn will help you avoid overreacting or acting out of insecurity.

Based on what I've learned throughout my careers, I see four phases in a leader's development as she copes with risk, power, and influence.

Phase 1: Knowing What You Don't Know

We all start out naïve. To move beyond this phase, you need to understand your company's corporate culture—how things work, how people communicate, how people take action. When I first became a vice-president at Texas Instruments, I believed that my bosses, peers, and subordinates would all be "on my side." *Very* naïve, right? I had to learn to quickly decide who was going to help and who wasn't, and to deal with people of both "persuasions." In my early days as a leader, I waited much too long to deal with people who either "wouldn't or couldn't" help me achieve my goals. Later on I learned to trust my gut or intuition, and found I was right most of the time.

Phase 2: Acquiring Credibility

As you learn what you don't know—and learn to move beyond it—the second stage is acquiring credibility. Among the key lessons now are working within the system, taking business risks, and building alliances and interpersonal networks. The core issue is doing what you say you'll do. Better yet, you need to exceed other people's expectations. You need to be identified as a "go-to" person. As you do so, you'll be recognized as someone with outstanding potential. Credibility is others' confidence that you'll get the job done right and on time. As you become seen as resourceful, resilient, and relentless, you'll acquire the credentials that make others want you to lead a team or a company.

Phase 3: A Style of Your Own

Over time, a woman starts to define a personal business style. By learning to delegate responsibilities, overcome obstacles, communicate clearly, and prove yourself reliable to allies, you determine and fine-tune your business style.

I received lots of feedback that I had a very good personal style and a strong ability to lead and manage. The strongest suit I had when starting at Cox was leadership. I wasn't a finance person, a marketer, or an engineer. My background was in Human Resources. But one thing I learned over time was that one of my strengths was what I'd mistaken earlier for a deficiency: I didn't have a particular leaning toward marketing, financial planning, or engineering. I viewed all recommendations, suggestions, and paths to achieving goals as equally worthy of consideration. I didn't have a predetermined bent toward any of those key functional areas. I wasn't even aware of this situation in the early stages, but it became a real strength in the longer term. Why? Because my team perceived my lack of bias as fairness . . . . But I couldn't be anything else because I didn't have any preconceived notions.

This situation doubles back to the issue of authenticity and definition of style. You have to take what you have and figure out how to make it work. Perhaps you don't have a particular expertise in what are generally considered the paths into senior leadership. On the other hand, if you possess what I mentioned earlier as the critical attributes of leadership—being resourceful, being a quick learner, and so forth—then you will find ways to leverage whatever functional expertise you possess. It's all about playing your strong suit and minimizing or making adjustments where you are short.

Phase 4: Taking Responsibility

One of the things I remember Jill telling me was: "You've got to be the big dog." Those were her exact words. She knew that I hadn't completely taken on that mantle of responsibility yet. To be honest, I knew what she meant, but I wasn't sure how to use it! I had the title, but I didn't *own* the job yet.

Ownership is the prerequisite to risk-taking, power, and influence. You need to be aware of that. If we're talking about power and influence, we have to ask, What are they? We need to distinguish between the two. Ultimately, power is about the potential of an individual or group to influence another individual or group. Influence is the exercise of power to change other people's behaviors or attitudes, or to get a group of people to do something they might not otherwise choose to do.

Needless to say, this is where all the networking and the relationships come in. If your relationships are weak or your networks are deficient, you will limit your capacity for power and influence. When you move into a senior position, you'll have to scramble to develop them. I know now that this is one of the reasons I struggled so greatly in my first leadership role when I first arrived at Cox. I was new to the function. The situation was tough. But I was good at decision-making, and I had some skills I'd brought with me from TI—skills that were somewhat unique to the industry. Among those skills were a deep knowledge of quality and customer focus, and some great tools for managing efficiency and effectiveness.

Sometimes women get a bit self-righteous and say something like, "I'm not going to use any of those dirty tricks. I won't rely on power and influence. I'm going to do this the right way—through my own good works, my knowledge, and my skill." Ethics and honesty are paramount, of course. However, it's important to acknowledge that risk-taking, power, and influence aren't inherently unethical. They aren't dirty tricks unless you make them into dirty tricks. They are simply the language of corporations at the highest levels. When you understand that, it will be much easier to maneuver in the gray areas.

IMAGE

Image isn't the most important element of a strong leader, but every strong leader should know the image she projects and should use it accordingly. To complicate matters, though, there really aren't a lot of good female "image models." This situation presents a serious challenge for women in the corporate world.

Let's explore this issue further. Think about the "image" of a successful CEO. Describe that person. The odds are that you'll envision a "Central Casting" executive: a tall, dapper, silver-haired fifty-something *male*. Now, describe the corresponding female image. You'll probably have a much, much harder time conjuring an image. The reason, unfortunately, is that in the image department, our culture comes up short. In recent years, we've seen a few more women who are persuasive as role models: think of Carly Fiorina, Meg Whitman, or Ursula Burns. Others will become evident over the years. But in the short term, this issue of image remains a problem that all female executives will face. So, with the image of the strong, rugged individualistic leader in our minds, how can women cope with that and find our own way?

Men and women alike need to understand that there's a broad scope of leadership styles. I believe that everyone should lead in his or

A New Paradigm for Ambitious Women

her own way. For Jack Welch, his style worked for him. If Jack Welch had tried to be someone other than himself, the effort wouldn't have worked. Jack Welch did phenomenal things at GE; however, his strong personality style isn't the only path. Another strong path—one that I mentioned earlier—is the *servant leader style*. There are many options between these two extremes. Some interesting research suggests that the benefits of servant leadership may last longer than the more assertive, even flamboyant styles. The big question is whether the benefits of a leader's guidance can continue after his or her tenure.

The core issue is being authentic—being true to yourself and doing what you do well, recognizing what your strengths are, and not trying to follow what someone else tells you or expects you to. Somewhere along the line, you have to figure out who *you* are and what *you* want to do, and what will be your best leadership style.

For instance, I surprised people at times because I didn't yell at people when they repeatedly didn't perform. If I asked someone to do something important, and if he or she failed at the assigned task repeatedly for no good reason, I simply fired the person. After a while, people learned that I might not raise my voice, but you really needed to listen to what I said because I really meant it.

For the time being, women will simply need to look within themselves and find the image that suits them best and that feels authentic. The good news: since there is no clear image for women, you can create your own. That bad news is essentially the same. The very best guidance I received on the subject of image was a great coach who asked me one day, "How do you show your passion?" It took me some time to find a way to show and articulate my passion to my team. But when I did, I also solidified my image in a very positive way.

BALANCING PERSONAL LIFE AND WORK LIFE

Another huge issue for women concerns balancing personal life and work. Balance is a concept that has undergone considerable change over the years. Twenty or twenty-five years ago, the focus was all about "achieving balance." The unspoken expectation was that if you got it right, balance would be just fine—and would stay that way. The thinking has now evolved. What matters most is the journey itself: you may have multiple destinations; it's all about the process of getting there, of expanding your thinking about balance.

As influenced by my experiences at the Betsy Magness Leadership Institute, I see two fundamental myths in our thinking about balance. One myth is that balance is a concept that's relevant only for married women with children. That's not the case. All women strive for balance. However, various aspects of the situation differ for different people. Married women who don't have children will face their own issues of balance and will need to address them creatively. So will unmarried women. The other myth is the notion of "having it all." Scores of books and countless magazine articles have been written on this topic! After many years of assuming that "having it all" meant achieving *all of your goals at the same time,* the newer thinking is that you can indeed have it all, but not necessarily by achieving all goals simultaneously. There may be stages of life when you emphasize one goal (such as rapid career development) while deemphasizing some other goal (such as meeting the constant demands of hands-on parenting when your children are young). There will be inevitable priorities, tradeoffs, and attendant satisfactions and frustrations. In any case, balance will be something that you achieve over the long haul, not as a single, permanent state of being. As one female CEO put it, "I hate this concept [of balance] when it means that I have to be a perfect mom and a perfect CEO every day. That's impossible—simply impossible." It's better to focus on the longer term, as opposed to trying to be totally balanced at every moment of every day throughout your career. What is important every day, however, is that you are in control of your own life, and not letting family, spouse, or work define you. You set the priorities and make the trade-offs that work best for you.

THE WALL AND THE GATE

One other inevitable feature of life at the top is the fear or uncertainty you feel—the fear that you are, after all, The Decider (as the second President Bush put it) and that (in the words of President Truman), "The buck stops here." Under these circumstances, it's inevitable that you will feel some degree of fear, loneliness, and uncertainty.

My response to this situation: consider it normal. Fear is inevitable. It won't go away; you'll have to learn to deal with it. Fear is a wall you'll face time after time. You probably won't lose the capacity for fear; it's simply part of being human. But although fear is a wall, that wall has a gate. The gate is courage. Courage doesn't eliminate fear, but it allows you to pass through it. Sometimes this happens simply because you're on the spot all the time and you have no choice but to pass through the gate—not once, not twice, but over and over and over again. Once you pass through for the first time, going through the wall of fear is significantly easier the next time. Does the process ever get "easy"? No. But you learn to recognize what fear looks like, and you recognize your ability to manage it—to cope with it and take action even though you may feel afraid or uncertain. I take great comfort in understanding all people deal with fear.

And loneliness? That's part of the job at the top. There will be critical times where you will need to make a decision or take an action that is unpopular or highly risky. As long as you have made the best decision possible, have honored your values, and have maintained your integrity, you will have gone as far as you can go. Most of the time you will win . . . but no one wins all the time. Take both the wins and occasional losses with the same degree of equanimity and grace. People will celebrate your wins and will support you when you need it.

I've heard a lot of women say, "Oh, I could never do that because of X." Generally, "X"—whatever that may be—is a result of fear. Pick a reason: "I'm not strong enough," "I'm not good enough," "I wouldn't be able to do that." But you never know until you try. One way of getting past fear is what I experienced during my early days at Cox Communications: by not having any choice! To switch metaphors: You just get thrown into the river. You have to learn to swim. However, you can learn from others as well. You can use relationships and networks to help meet your goals.

I believe the most unfortunate women are the ones who never try . . . the ones who allow others to make their decisions and define their paths. If you never pass through the gate and conquer the wall, you will always wonder "what could have been." My very wise father once told me you should make all your life decisions as though you are 70 years old and looking back on your life. I'm pretty sure that my only regret will be not taking enough risks as opportunities presented themselves.

Find your courage and move past your wall. It will be the best thing you ever do for yourself. Start today.

CHAPTER 7

THE RESPONSIBILITY AND ACCOUNTABILITY OF MEN

The goal I've described throughout this book is straightforward: for women to thrive in the C Suite in ways that fully recognize, utilize, and reward their talents, skills, knowledge, and abilities as evidenced by their representation. Achieving this goal will come about substantially from women's own efforts, but not without the full awareness and support of men. So this raises the question: what about men? Where do men fit into the picture, both in positive and negative ways? How can female executives enlist men's talents and power for the good of women's careers?

RESPONSIBILITY AND ACCOUNTABILITY

In my view, the answer to these questions starts with an understanding of responsibility and accountability. The CEO of a corporation is responsible and accountable for the ultimate successes or failures of the corporation. Where men are in charge, they are responsible and accountable. Where women are in charge, they are responsible and accountable. In fact, I can't imagine a CEO who would want it to be any other way. We should define these terms, however, before we discuss the implications further.

Are responsibility and accountability different? Of course they are, though initially they may look quite similar. *Responsibility*, in the broadest sense, is the formal or informal ownership of actions and results. If you are the CEO of a corporation, you are responsible for everything that happens within that corporation as the business grows and develops. Even if you didn't have a direct hand in a specific outcome, you are still responsible for the people, processes, and procedures that produce the results. "The buck stops here"—and *here* is your own desk.

By contrast, *accountability* is the report card that measures how well you have succeeded, as well as the extent of your success or failure with regard to the corporation's progress on your watch. Accountability is the quantifiable dimensions of responsibility. If you are responsible, you've already said, "The buck stops here"—and now you provide the documentation in terms of P&L statements, opinions, and directives. You can't have responsibility without accountability, and you can't be fully accountable for something if you don't accept responsibility for it.

What I consider most important regarding this chapter is that whoever may be in charge—whether that person is male or female—the leader is both responsible and accountable. I can't imagine any competent CEO *not* acknowledging total responsibility and accountability for the success or failure of the company on his or her watch. The CEO may not be personally responsible for the individual success of every single person, since personal responsibility and accountability by these other individuals is also a crucial element in their success. However, a CEO is responsible for providing equal opportunity and tools to get the job done, as well as for insuring that steps are taken to clear any obstacles that get in the way. How, then, do CEO's or boards measure the success of their companies with regard to the overall success of women? They do so just as they measure any other outcome: by the numbers. If the numbers are not there, no amount of "good faith" or "activity" suffices. You either get it done or you don't.

The Implications for Men and Women

Are there differences between women's and men's accountability and responsibility for the lack of women leading our corporations? Yes, but only because of the numbers. As we've noted, less than 4% of current CEOs are women. Only 15% of the executives one level down are women. If the numbers were 50/50, 60/40, or even 70/30, the question of responsibility and accountability wouldn't be such a big deal. But since the numbers are 96/4, where does this ratio leave us? I've thought long and hard about this question. Here's how I see it. Women executives are chiefly responsible for putting the issue of their role in the C Suite on the table and keeping it there. What's more, they are responsible for keeping the issue front-and-center in a manner that is proactive and positive—and business-oriented. The question is: for how long do women work only within the corporation for making positive, visible change, and what happens when the company isn't responsive? When and why should women be prepared to seek remedies outside their own corporation?

What about men? Men are responsible and accountable for being fully active in redressing the challenges that female executives face, as well as for women's meager representation in the C-Suite, as well as on boards. Since men are in 96% of the top posts, they need to take specific and measurable steps to correct the imbalance. The bottom line: men and women share responsibility and accountability. What is measured is what gets done. If having representative numbers of women in places of power isn't part of a corporation's agenda, it won't be acted on. Currently, this goal isn't a business imperative in most companies because the people in power—generally speaking, men—simply haven't made this agenda a priority. Because men don't put this issue where it can be measured and acted on, nothing happens. Men and women must both recognize that repeating past initiatives and practices isn't likely to produce different results. Change starts by squarely facing the reality that the CEO and the board must take personal responsibility and accountability for success.

The more I think about the situation, the more I recall again what my mother used to say about marriage. She said, "Sweetheart, if you give 150 percent and your husband also gives 150 percent—and if you're real lucky—your marriage will probably work out." This situation holds true with men's and women's responsibility in the corporate sphere. Both men and women will have to go far above and beyond what might be expected to make the necessary changes. It means that men will have to do things in a very overt and positive manner. Women are going to have to do the same. If everyone makes this level of commitment, the situation will get significantly better. If not, it's hard to see how substantive change will be forthcoming.

FOSTERING CHANGE

Our discussion now arrives at an interesting dilemma. I've said that if placing women in the upper reaches of the power hierarchy isn't part of a corporation's agenda, it probably just won't happen.

A New Paradigm for Ambitious Women

And, unfortunately, placing more than a few women in power generally isn't an issue that many CEOs consider important. How, then, can other executives—maybe a level or two down in the hierarchy—foster this agenda?

The short answer: it won't be easy. However, if the issue in a given corporation is chiefly a lack of awareness, there may be some ways that women and men at lower levels of an organization can foster change. An interesting example concerns Tom Engibous, the CEO of Texas Instruments who took over during the time period after I'd left the company. At one point, I'm told, Tom attended a meeting of the women's network group at TI, and he was impressed by how this group of women executives functioned. He immediately contacted his VP for HR, who happened to be male, and Tom said, "We will know we have been successful when our women can act in our management and senior meetings as they were acting here." So for Tom, the issue was awareness. During his tenure, the number of women executives increased significantly at TI. Sometimes awareness can prompt change, even dramatic change. I believe that awareness is where we start—a different and higher level of awareness than we've had up till now. Specifically, what we need is new level of awareness by men, starting with a candid, thorough look at goals, progress to date, actions, and accountability. We've made some progress, but we're far from finished. In fact, the most difficult phase may lie ahead. Why? Because the awareness and accountability is now about the very space that CEOs and board members occupy. It's easier to prescribe "fixes" for everyone else in the corporation. Everyone *has* done his or her job to a greater or lesser degree. It's now time for the leadership—men and women alike—to address difficult truths and to accept responsibility and accountability for change in the C Suite.

At the other end of the spectrum of actions, you have political pressures that can be brought to bear. I mentioned earlier that when I was still at TI, a group of women formed what I'll call a business coalition, and they basically challenged the corporation to help them foster positive, business-oriented change for women within TI. While they took action in a positive, proactive manner, the unspoken threat was the possibility of unionizing. There was a huge fear among the top executives at the time that these women might do precisely that. So, yes, political pressure can be effective. The women did a beautiful job of not directly threatening anyone; instead, they used their collective power and influence to bring about positive change for the company—and for themselves as well. The fact that the women in charge were some of the best and brightest technical minds carried a huge amount of weight with the senior male executives. The situation simply couldn't be overlooked or treated lightly.

Beyond that, there's the option of legal redress. Wal-Mart, for instance, was recently embroiled in a class-action lawsuit filed by female employees who claimed that the company had discriminated against them in terms of wages and promotions. This lawsuit went all the way up to the U.S. Supreme Court. Legal redress is tricky, however; while it is certainly a way to get things done, it's complicated and expensive, and it generally creates hard feelings. Moreover, this approach takes a long time to prompt any new outcomes. Lawsuits take years to work their way through the courts, and even a successful outcome for the plaintiffs may not lead to immediate change. However, even negative legal outcomes can trigger positive internal changes within a company.

To summarize: if you're trying to foster change, you have basically three options. Awareness and resulting transformation is the first and best. Second is using political pressures within the corporation.

The third is legal redress. I believe that overall, fostering awareness is the best approach. The TI women, for instance, did a phenomenal job of bringing pressure within the company, and their success was partly a result of acting in a positive, proactive manner. By doing so, they made the path to change easier for all to accept and implement. While the women took a big risk, they had faith in the overall character and integrity of the company, and they wanted their success to be TI's success and vice versa. Likewise, the leadership at TI took a deep breath, examined some long held beliefs, and took action. In looking back at that time, I believe both sides gave 150%. And this willingness to make a commitment truly worked.

Women and Non-linear Careers

One of the beliefs that I know gets used against women executives is that because of our less-linear career paths, we are perceived as having less commitment than men do and less willingness to give our full attention to our jobs. Also, compared to a man's career path, a woman's path may show slower progress and more gaps. However, this less linear path should *not* automatically brand the woman the lesser candidate. We must move beyond the belief that the shortest and most direct route to the top is the only and best route. Boards and top-level executives may rely on this argument not so much because they are willfully biased against women but because they truly believe that a "fast tracker" who has risen quickly through the ranks is the most promising. Is this argument valid? I'm not convinced of that. You don't need an uninterrupted career path to be a talented executive, to understand how a corporation works, or to grasp what's needed to thrive in the marketplace. What troubles me even more, however, is the implicit argument that fast track "insiders" are best suited for the C Suite. I would argue that the opposite is often true: outsiders' views are often especially constructive and unbiased. And I believe that many executives know this to be true.

I've been intrigued over a period of many years, for instance, how often companies bring in "someone from the outside" when their business is in trouble. One example is the emergency restructuring of General Motors a few years ago. Practically the first words that Ed Whitaker spoke in public were: "I don't know anything about cars." Since then, GM has reversed its downward trajectory and seems on the way to renewed success. GM needed someone who had leadership expertise *outside* the industry. This situation disproves the claim that all CEOs must have a linear career. There's nothing wrong with a linear career, but it isn't the only way to gain expertise. If this weren't the case, executives wouldn't go outside the company during severe business conditions. Companies with long-term sustainable success also know this truth. The Catalyst organization has studies that demonstrate, for instance, that diverse companies have more long-term success than companies that are less diverse.

My own personal history is another example. I wasn't a cable veteran, and I'd spent all my work life in a "soft" support job until Jill asked me, "What can you do?" Jill supported me in all the appropriate ways, but she gave me the wonderful gift of trusting my unconventional background. She trusted me to use my outsider's knowledge to foster change—and I did just that.

How can executives change attitudes about nonlinear careers? I'm not entirely sure, but I believe that the timing in the United States is now perfect for starting this discussion. Why? Because we've seen the near-collapse of our entire financial and economic system. People in the financial institutions, as well as in other business sectors, now understand that better checks and balances might well have prevented us from driving right up to the precipice. Those checks and balances might have come from a more diverse group of people making decisions. By "diverse" I don't mean necessarily *just* in terms of racial, ethnic, or gender makeup; rather, I mean diverse in terms of thoughts, backgrounds, and approaches. Diversity of these sorts might have avoided the mindsets that fogged many people's perceptions of the risks so many organizations were taking. And when I say diverse, I mean truly diverse. I don't know how many times I've sat in a room with all white men who have all worked for the same company, have the same backgrounds, and still assert they are "diverse." And somehow they genuinely believed it.

Some corporations still proceed as if they are waging a military campaign. But running a business isn't necessarily analogous to the military. In making this statement, I don't mean to say that you should be any less competitive or any less intense in your efforts. Rather, I mean that your decision-making can be more variable in nature. The armed services understandably rely on a strict chain of command to function; by contrast, many (if not most) businesses are likely to thrive by using a more complex and varied approach to decision making, communications, and thinking. You need to look at different approaches to solving problems. You need people with many different modes of thought. To have the best car company in the country, for instance, you need to learn not just from long-time experts from the auto industry. You need people with wide experience in the retail industry. You need experts who are IT professionals. You need experts in the field of electronic media. And you need to listen to your customers, the majority of whom are women. In short, you need intellectual diversity. And this wide range of experience and insight will be more easily attained if you open the C Suite to more women *precisely because women often have less conventional, less linear, more varied ranges of business and different life experiences.*

Earlier in this book, when I described my career at Cox Communications, I said that I was inexperienced. I was—in terms of that specific company. But I actually knew a lot. In entering the cable industry, I brought insights to the table that Cox desperately needed even if people in the company didn't know it—and perhaps I didn't know it, either, at that exact moment. I brought a much deeper understanding of quality as an integral part of doing business. I brought a systems support understanding to Cox. I helped change how they ran their IT organization. In truth, I didn't know anything about IT—but I knew that this factor was crucial to how we would run our business, so I hired someone knowledgeable to take that role. Cox also didn't understand much about centralized organizational design. Why do you need 40 identical units when you can have 20 with half the cost? So, one reason that I managed to do so well at Cox was that I had great mentors; but I also had knowledge and skills that enabled me to take action in ways that a long-time cable person wouldn't have brought to the position. Someone like that would've continued to do the same things in the same way. If so, the organization might have failed. But my unit at Cox didn't fail. On the contrary, we turned the situation around and succeeded.

WHERE THIS LEAVES US

We have no choice now but to return to the very start of our discussion. Whoever is in power has responsibility and accountability. Those in power are chiefly men. Therefore, men are the people responsible and accountable for change in the area we've been discussing. But let's switch for a moment to an analogy from the science of physics—specifically, an analogy that draws from the nature of momentum. An object at rest will tend to stay at rest. An object in motion will tend to stay in motion. I believe that these laws of physics are applicable to change in the corporate world. Substantial change rarely happens in a corporation unless someone at the top exerts some force to move an object at rest. Culture change and dramatic shifts are almost always driven from the top. If the people at the top want something to happen, it will tend to become a reality to a greater or lesser degree. If the people at the top don't want it to happen, or if they just ignore the situation, change is unlikely. CEOs and other senior executives have very broad power and influence. What happens as a result of that power and influence is the ability to get things done. Because men have the power, they should be taking more responsibility for fostering this process we have discussed throughout my book. If they do so, change will occur. I have no doubt about this. I also believe that most CEOs know that there are many qualified women out there. All they have to do is make it a priority and measure their progress.

So, to close this chapter, I will end with a challenge to our male executive peers:

Guys, if you're going to be part of this process, you have to be part of it *at the top*. You have to say, "Okay, this is important. This is what needs to happen. And this is what we're going to do. It's time to recognize we need revolutionary change, not evolutionary improvement. We need a transformational quest.

You need us women and our talents. The business world needs us and what we have to offer.

Take a stand.

CHAPTER 8

EXECUTIVE WOMEN IN THEIR OWN WORDS

Throughout this book so far, I have focused on presenting my views about women in the C Suite and my recommendations for how to advance women's careers. I've based these views and recommendations on my several decades of work in the corporate world, on my extensive readings of both technical and mainstream writings on this topic, and on past and present interactions with business leaders throughout the country. Readers will have noted that I have strong opinions and blunt-spoken suggestions on these issues! That being said, I'm aware that women throughout the corporate world have their own varied experiences, their own insights, their own opinions, and their own suggestions as we all move forward. I welcome and celebrate the variety of these women's perceptions and ideas, many of which have shaped my own beliefs in important ways.

For this reason, I want to shift the focus now from my own viewpoint to those of other women. This chapter will present six highly accomplished, deeply insightful executives and will "turn over the microphone" so they can express their own insights about the topics I've presented throughout this book. As you will undoubtedly notice, these six women have a wide range of backgrounds, experiences, career paths, concerns, perceptions, and suggestions. Some of these observations and suggestions overlap from one person to another. Others are specific to one person's own experiences. Some are consistent with my own views; others are at variance. Regarding all of them, however, I deeply admire what they have achieved, and I celebrate the diversity of their backgrounds, goals, and accomplishments. This diversity is truly the point: there are thousands of women out there in corporate America—tens of thousands—who are qualified to ascend higher up the leadership ladder; they have greatly varied abilities, aspirations, and goals; and the sheer variety of what they have to offer is a vast resource that this country's business sector can't afford to ignore or bypass. For these reasons, I want to give this fascinating selection of women executives a forum to comment on what they have experienced and how they view the issues.

What follows is a very brief intro to each woman, then an excerpt of questions and answers drawn from much longer interviews I've undertaken during the course of writing this book. These women are so insightful and eloquent that I want simply to let them speak for themselves.

Please note: to ensure these executives' personal privacy, I have changed five of the six names and altered the details of backgrounds and employment for those five. (The exception is Iris Newalu, Director of Smith College Executive Education for Women.)

A New Paradigm for Ambitious Women

MARISSA

Senior Vice President at a large corporation, Marissa has worked in her industry for several decades.

CONNIE: Let's talk about the core issues. Less than 4 percent of the Fortune 1000 CEOs are women, and if you go one level down to executives—admittedly a somewhat nebulous title—only 15.6 percent of people with that rank are women. Those numbers haven't changed much since the late 1990's. As an executive woman, do you think this is an important business issue?

MARISSA: I absolutely think it's important. I'm a woman, so I'm going to give you the woman's point of view on having grown up in the business world. I do think it's important, one, because you think about the buying power in the United States particularly is women. And the [overall] population isn't 15 percent women—it's predominantly women. So if you're in business, you really have to be thinking about who your audience is, and if your leadership doesn't reflect that, then that's a big problem. But it has to be a little more dramatic than that. I think that as a CEO or as a board, you have to insist that you will grow and have certain percentages of both women and people of color. You can't just have 5 percent. You can't just have 10 percent. It's got to be an equal footing at the table.

CONNIE: Are you stating that it needs to be not only an emphatic policy, but emphatic follow-through?

MARISSA: There have to be consequences if that doesn't occur—and rewards if it does. Diversity is lovely *if* you already have a lot of varied people in your organization. We may give a diversity award to a system who has shown a lot of progress in that area, particularly at the leadership level, so there's some reward for that, but not enough to make you say, "Yeah, this is really important in our company."

CONNIE: Do you think that the activity around diversity and inclusion has become a place where lots of activity happens, but everybody kind of knows that it's not really going to change the status quo?

MARISSA: I think people feel good if you have diversity councils and you're able to talk more openly about differences, and I think that has been helpful in the workplace. Now they feel a little more comfortable with that, so that's a good thing. But in terms of actually making movement in sheer numbers of people in decision-making power or—no, I don't think anybody thinks that's the case here.

CONNIE: Let's talk about mentoring. Does it matter if your mentors are men or women?

MARISSA: It should be a combination of both. But I really think it's important to have men mentors if you're a woman, in particular because they're going to have a different lens and tell you what they're going to look for as a CEO or an executive in a company.

CONNIE: Do you feel that men are partial to mentoring other men? And if so, why?

MARISSA: Yes, because men are familiar. Look, if you're going to hire somebody on your inner circle team, you've got to be really comfortable with them personally as well. And so I think that that just goes that way because they go, "Oh, here's a guy.

A New Paradigm for Ambitious Women

He's like me. We can go to lunch, we can play golf," and it's all subconscious about that. And they get together, and there's no weirdness in the group to them. I'm perfectly comfortable with my team and I have one woman and four guys, and I'm perfectly comfortable with them.

CONNIE: Men seem willing to mentor and champion women to a certain level, then it stops.

MARISSA: Right. And did they really want—do they want to take that stand? Is that what they want to spend their time on? Or do they want to spend it on business and making money? And when you go out on Wall Street with that, if that's what they're talking about the whole time, mentoring women ain't going to get them a better stock price for any of us.

CONNIE: How can we make change happen? And if we don't set goals, will change ever happen?

MARISSA: Well, it has to happen with men. It's not us women who are going to make it happen. The men have to make it happen. Women like me are not going to make those changes.

CONNIE: What about the issue of balance? To what degree is balancing work and personal life part of the problem for women?

MARISSA: At the end of the day women get frustrated and they say, "Really? Do I want to do this?" How do you balance it? Well, you don't very well because you go home, and the man generally isn't going to be like my husband was—willing to take the kids to school and decide to support your career. No, they generally have a pretty big career, too. So not only do you do that, but you come home, and you're the one who still has to figure out what to pack for lunch, put the kids to bed. So really then what's in it for us? What satisfaction do we get at the end of the day?

CONNIE: Is there anything else from a personal standpoint that you would want to say that would give insights into what a woman should do?

MARISSA: One thing that does disturb me is that women still aren't really supportive of other women. Especially young women. My daughter is going into the HR world, and her boss just does not support her at all. That's very disturbing to me to see that trend. We're very competitive, and we have enough problems trying to get men to promote us without having to deal with our own sex trying to derail us. So I don't know what we do about that one, but I'm starting to see that more and more. The other trend is women are opting out. I'm really seeing a lot of my friends and a lot of younger women saying, "My friends and I don't really want to go through all that." One woman said, "I'm real proud of you, but I don't want to have to climb up and try to get through that glass ceiling. That's just not appealing to me."

CONNIE: They're opting out by not proceeding with their own careers, or they're bailing out altogether?

MARISSA: They're happy just at a mid-level, and they don't want to run the world. They don't want to do more.

CONNIE: For women who don't have in-house mentoring, where do programs like the Betsy Magness Leadership Institute or the Smith Leadership Program fit in fostering confidence among women?

MARISSA: They are very important. The program is one thing, but it's also the support group. It's those other women that I think help them get there. So programs are fine, but it really has to be the people that you work with, that you are in your life with. If you marry somebody who doesn't value that, or doesn't think that your career is important, you're in trouble.

ANNALEE

After two previous careers—first in journalism, then in a job with a Texas Chamber of Commerce—Annalee shifted into an executive position in a large cable company. She has worked in that industry ever since.

CONNIE: Let's talk about mentoring. Did your mentor guide you specifically as a woman he wanted to empower, or was his mentoring gender-neutral—he just saw you as talented and, therefore, he was going to provide positive input?

ANNALEE: I think it was gender-neutral, in that I know he mentored other people on staff as well. But I didn't see the world in gender terms until much later in my career, and I don't see it in those terms today, as some women seem to. That's just not a natural filter for me. I also don't think he was mentoring me on purpose. He could only be as successful as the people on his staff because there was too much work to be done. And so it was only by his ego and his own ambition that he felt the need to mentor us, so that we could help him succeed.

CONNIE: If I asked you to name three things that would need to change in the workplace to significantly improve the numbers for women in the C Suite, what comes to mind?

ANNALEE: I really think a lot of it is leadership development, for women but also for men, and about helping leaders see how better decisions result from the vetting of diverse viewpoints in the workplace. But you asked for three things. So, top on the list is authentic leadership development. Second is mentoring. Last is the whole notion that information is power and the value of sharing of information.

CONNIE: If you could take a magic wand and make women have all the leadership characteristics they need, and if men and women understood one another, do you think that would then substantially change the needle?

ANNALEE: Not really. When I think about why I've been able to move up in the organization, it is because at every step along the way I was able to persuade my boss that he or she could trust me. And not just that I was going to be truthful, but that I would have his back, take one for the team, help her manage up the ladder, put on a poker face in defending his decisions whether or not I agreed with them. The boss has to know you "get it" about the big picture and the long view.

CONNIE: Do you remember how you learned to do that? Did you learn it by yourself, or were there other men and/or women who helped you see that?

ANNALEE: I don't know. I was never able to articulate that until I went through the Betsy Magness Leadership Institute. Men and women who succeed have figured out that you have to put the company's interests front and center. And obviously I knew that before BMLI or I wouldn't have been there, but I had not articulated it before. I feel like I always knew about the team mentality. Maybe it comes from being the youngest of five, where my siblings taught me how to keep secrets from Mom when it was in everyone's best interest to do so. That's where I learned to solve problems at the lowest level possible. That's where I learned it's about the long haul, not today's trip.

CONNIE: What can be done that will foster men's trust of women in high positions?

ANNALEE: I think people trust people who they know are going to do what it takes for the company and for them. So I think it's not just that they don't trust women—I think they don't trust some men. The difference is that women have to prove themselves worthy to men, whereas men are trusted until they prove themselves unworthy. Mid-level in my career, at a company retreat at which I was the only woman on the management team, we were smoking cigars and playing poker together. And it helps that I naturally like cigars and poker, because I think that retreat changed the way they saw me. If it had been inauthentic, it would have hurt, not helped. But because it was authentic, it gave them a basis for viewing me differently. But I did have to prove to them that if they told me something, I would be discreet, I would use that information properly and wisely. That they saw me as "one of them" helped me gain their trust.

CONNIE: How do you handle the dichotomy in your mind? You said earlier that men are trusted until they prove they can't be trusted, and women have almost the reverse of that—they have to prove they can be trusted. And some women have to prove it over and over and over again.

ANNALEE: We do. How do I deal with that? I just accept that that is the way it is. And I pay attention to the things over which I have control—my own patterns of trust.

CONNIE: If you look back through your career, are there factors where being a woman has hindered your career?

ANNALEE: There's never a time where I didn't get a job or I didn't get a promotion or I didn't get an opportunity and I could clearly point to the fact that it was because I was a woman. I applied and I interviewed for one position, and I thought the job was mine. Then at the very last minute I didn't get the job, and a man did, but it never occurred to me that he got that job because he was a man. What I believed, and still believe, is that he got that job because he knew the hiring executive really well. But I don't look backward and I could analyze it forever.

CONNIE: You were frequently the only or one of the few women at whatever level? Did you ever feel isolated?

ANNALEE: No, because I was connected to the team, they just happened to be guys. I was one of the guys from childhood on, so I was comfortable in that world. There is more isolation in my current field than in previous fields. Sadly, there's still a lot of activity centered around hunting, fishing, and golf.

CONNIE: From a personal standpoint, can you talk about the balance of marriage and life and kids? As you look back, would you do it all again?

A New Paradigm for Ambitious Women

ANNALEE: Yes, I would, but there are things that I wish I had known earlier, mainly the importance of taking care of myself. I didn't have time—correction, I didn't *make* time—to exercise. I wish I had known earlier the correlation between health and energy. And also—this is a bit of a personal story—when my husband and I were in one of the inevitable dips in any marriage, he said to me, "Look, I'm very proud of you as a professional, and I'm in awe of what you're able to accomplish. I know that you have demands on your time outside of the normal workweek. But once in a while you need to choose me. Not all the time, but once in a while." That was a major turning point—for me to realize balance wasn't on any given day; it was a balance over time of choices, and that sometimes you have to make the choice to be with family, just as sometimes you have to make the choice to be away from family.

CONNIE: One of the things that concerns me is the perception that careers have to be linear, and that if you take time out for a baby or anything else, you are losing time. What are your thoughts about that issue?

ANNALEE: We, as women, have done ourselves a disservice in talking about career ladders, as opposed to career journeys. The whole notion of a journey didn't occur to me till I participated in the Betsy Magness Leadership Institute, so I thought I was on a ladder and I didn't know I was on a winding path. We need to change the terminology. Stop talking about ladders or even the current use of lattice. I think if we let women and men set off on a life journey, not start climbing a ladder, then we would all be happier and more balanced. If a career decision were merely a fork in the road—and not a step up, down, or off a ladder—we would be less anguished about those decisions. Of course, the hiring process has to change to give people a chance to explain their forks in the road, rather than dismiss non-linear careers.

I also think women generally are not good at making a decision before we have all the information. So when we are at that fork in the road we tend to hesitate—we won't take a job before we know if we can do it, or leap before we really know what is around the corner. At a critical juncture in my career, I was thrust in a position of taking on a role I had little experience doing and even less training for. I flat didn't know what I was doing. A male colleague said to me, "Treat it like an audition. Just act the part while you're doing your homework, and you'll figure it out before anyone knows you were temporarily faking it." I don't know why somebody had to tell me that, but they did. And I think women are more likely than men to feel like it's somehow wrong to agree to do something you've never done before or aren't absolutely ready for. I'm not saying you should misrepresent your skills or experience; just trust yourself at least as much as the person who is trusting you enough to offer the job!

IRIS NEWALU

Over the past ten years, Iris Newalu has directed Smith College Executive Education for Women, a consortium of leadership programs for women at Smith College in Northampton, Massachusetts.

CONNIE: Please tell us about the programs for women executives at Smith College.

IRIS: We have grown a portfolio of programs. I like to say that we specialize in one thing and one thing only. What Smith does well is strategic leadership development for women. We're not a business school, and we don't try to be. We really have built our programs on that fact. Frankly, I think that gives us a lot of leverage and a lot of flexibility to go out there and hire the best faculty we can find. We're not married to any particular research, background, or faculty, and I see that again and again as a benefit.

CONNIE: I've looked at probably a hundred leadership programs for women. My impression is that they're good, but they miss the mark. They talk about networking, but they don't really get down to the nitty-gritty of really understanding what enduring relationships are all about.

IRIS: We understand how to create a learning environment that really supports women. Our research tells us that regardless of where women work, they come to their jobs and to leadership roles with common experiences and concerns and beliefs and issues. Sometimes they just don't have good female role models around them, so they do experience that isolation in their jobs. They feel that their needs aren't being addressed in more traditional, male-oriented leadership programs. They have a few receptions at night where the program organizers say, "Okay, go out there and network." That's not what we do. You have to do a whole lot more than that. And so we try to create places where women can learn with their true professional peers.

So, as I said, we specialize in strategic leadership development of women at all stages of the organization—from emerging managers to senior level global managers. One of the values is that the participants are true peers. They're sitting there across the table from somebody, maybe from a completely different industry. We have a woman from a pharmaceutical company sitting across from a woman from Wall Street, and initially they might say, "What do we have in common?" But the more they get into the issues, the more they see how they are the same. The underlying factor here is that they're peers and that they have the same level of responsibility. They can truly talk and exchange. This creates a learning environment with their peers. There are special bonds of connection and trust that build up. That encourages risk-taking and collaborative group learning. And this results from women basically connecting with each other and sharing their experiences.

CONNIE: How do you see the current situation for executive women overall?

IRIS: I do think we're at a point where the time is right for women. There's a tipping point—something is happening. We are in dire times as far as the economy, but I do think that women are stepping up, and they are next in line. Let's face it, there's going to be a lot of retirement going on here pretty soon at the top. I was in a meeting a few months ago at one of our Ivy League schools. A professor who does global strategy work made this prediction: "In ten years, what I see for the structure is the women will be at the top governing the companies."

CONNIE: Does Smith track participants' progress through their organizations?

IRIS: I would love to say that we are able to track them all, but we just can't. We do follow up with our companies, who track their participants in the programs to study where the women are today, what advances they've made, and how their contribution is being seen. Our clients—especially the companies that have been connected with us for years—are doing their own internal tracking, and what they see are the retention rates and the performance reviews. Those are the two areas that they have been able to really hone in and see improvements. So two-thirds of the women who come to the program show improved retention and performance evaluations.

CONNIE: The current corporate structure was designed by men for men. Do you spend much time talking to the Smith participants about that?

IRIS: Our programs are gender-specific for the reason that we believe there is still a place for women to learn with other women and to be able to talk to each other about the issues they face every day in the workplace. That of course includes corporate structure and how most of those structures were based on a model that suited men in the fifties. However, today I do see many good companies working on being more flexible within some of those structures, to accommodate not only women but also the younger generations coming into the workforce. It turns out that that structure really isn't working anymore for a lot of people, not just women.

We have many discussions around what is working and what isn't, but it's not necessarily targeted in the curriculum. In every program we hold a senior executive women's panel, in which the participants have the opportunity to ask their questions about barriers and obstacles faced by senior executives who have been challenged and are meeting that challenge in their own careers. It's a very lively and candid session that opens new perspectives and ideas for the women on how to go forth and deal with their own challenges. Plus, we do teach them to be more politically savvy, understand the rules of engagement and how to negotiate for what they want and need to be successful. Through these tools they learn how to play the game better and stay in there.

CONNIE: Where do men fit into the picture of these programs?

IRIS: Part of our approach to women's leadership is to create culture change. We see our mission as developing future change agents who will work along with the men who want change, too, to create the workforce of tomorrow, where equality, flexibility, and collaboration are seen more as the norm. Men definitely fit into this picture. Women can't change all alone; we have to work together on this. And in some of our companies we have begun to offer an all-men's program to address some of the issues men are facing in the 21st century workplace. They are looking at what it means to be a man in corporate America today. Men are facing a lot of change as well and we are trying to help them navigate the change that is coming.

CONNIE: Can you give us an example of how the women-only format works for your participants?

IRIS: In the program about three years ago, there was a woman, who had been twenty-four years in a large pharmaceutical company. She's an M.D. and the head of her laboratory. She oversees forty people, mostly men. She asked a question in the morning, and the faculty, who really just loved her question, took off and had a great discussion. At lunch I was sitting next to her, and I said, "That was a great question. Look, people are still talking about it." And she said, "You know, I've been wanting to ask that question for about two years." I said, "Why haven't you before that?" Here she is, an M.D. and the head of her laboratory, and she has been around a long time now. Why hasn't this woman asked her question? She said, "It's fear of looking stupid. There's a double bind for me. I'm the lead, I'm the woman, I'm a scientist, and I'm supposed to have these answers. All these people are looking to me. This is the first place where I've felt safe enough to ask that question and really explore it."

CONNIE: Do you talk about very successful women and their marriages or life partnerships?

IRIS: Yes, we believe it is extremely relevant to address success, what that means, and how it affects our life choices, whether it be our marriages and families or other life obligations that come into every woman's life. We take a holistic view, because people do not *only* bring their minds to work, they bring their whole selves. So how women take care of themselves and manage their lives and energy is very important. Or they find themselves crumbling under the weight of their own success. Everyone is stressed today. But women deal with stress differently than men and they need to know how to handle it better. We have a session on self-care and women's health issues and get them motivated to make the kind of changes in their lives that will give them the energy and enthusiasm they need to have to live their life. It's always a very impactful session, I think because it touches such a deep nerve. They're so busy taking care of others, women almost need permission to take care of themselves.

CONNIE: Can you offer some thoughts about women and networking?

IRIS: Women are great networkers once they realize how important it truly is to their success. Women just don't always value it enough. And they often don't recognize how to break into the kind of networks that they need to be a part of. We integrate networking into our programs strategically, and in a way that fosters a natural kind of networking that gives women a chance to see where it could lead for them. Professional networking has to be strategic, but people won't do it if they don't understand the importance of it. After being in our programs, women tell me that they have created a far deeper and richer network to stay connected with then they ever had. And we reinforce this with our own follow up engagements to keep them connected.

JENELLE

An initial career in public education shifted several decades ago into a position in the corporate communications office at a private insurance company. Jenelle has worked in that sector until a year ago.

CONNIE: Could you comment on to the degree to which your industry nurtures women and brings women up through the ranks?

JENELLE: Historically it's been dreadful. Then, in the late 1980's, the company noticed and has worked harder to fix that. In our division there were a fair number of women, all at the same level, yet the management was completely male in my division and at the top of the organization. And all a sudden some women started rattling the cages upstairs, and the chairman at the time suddenly promoted a bunch of women in order to balance it.

A New Paradigm for Ambitious Women

CONNIE: Has there been improvement since then?

JENELLE: Yeah, I think so. I still feel as though it's an improvement because it's measured now. It didn't used to be. There's a measurement and it's in managers' goals to make sure that there is a diverse staff in all ways.

CONNIE: Can you talk a little bit about exactly what the women early on did when they rattled the cages?

JENELLE: A couple of things stand out. One is that the senior women were not role models for the rest of us. I didn't even see them as women. They seemed to have gotten to where they arrived by acting like men—not being very nurturing. You remember the outfits with bow ties? That whole thing. And I remember thinking of the five women who were above me at the time: wow, I don't want to aspire to be any of these people. And so the first couple of generations of high-level promotions were people that I felt like were smart but tough broads. They just didn't feel like me at all. So one of the ways that they rattled cages was to mask the ways that they thought might be threatening to men. So rather than use feminine wiles, which ironically seems to be back in vogue these days, they took away some of the things that might've seemed threatening by almost neutering themselves. That's one thing.

Then there was a women's action council—a group of outspoken women who did not have a great reputation when the group was first formed. Then it grew, and it started getting sponsors of male executives, which was a good thing, actually. And somebody along the way got them to focus on business issues. Over the years, this group held a kind of summit for middle managers, and there are probably 150 people there, with snazzy speakers and business-minded workshops. It's a group that has grown and become widely recognized; it's an honor to be invited to it; and it's an honor to lead it or be the co-leader. I think it's well established to the point where I feel as though there is greater awareness of diversity or of women's issues woven in the fabric of the organization. My feeling is let's stop bifurcating men and women and start looking at other issues.

One other issue stands out. One of the sessions was having people talk about who gave them a helping hand. So maybe five or six women volunteered, more maybe, to tell a story about the person who really made a difference in their career, and every one of them talked about a man. And my answer would've been a man as well. And that is the part about the women's story that I think is well known but unspoken: which is that women don't really help each other very much.

CONNIE: Is that because the women have too many pressures on them to become mentors? Or is there an element of competition with other women? Or both?

JENELLE: I think it is those two things and one more, which is self-confidence. Confident people, whether men or women, are comfortable creating space for others. Those who are uncertain of their standing, or their future, definitely don't have time for other people. So they might convey confidence, or even believe that they are self-confident, but to me it's only manifested when someone makes space for you. So I have always worked for men until a few years ago. So now I've worked for two women for the first time in my life and learned a lot in that experience.

I would say that that's when I formed my philosophy about confidence. The first woman I worked for, one of the smartest people I've ever met, had a capacity for information and ideas that is just unrivaled, which made it tough because she was on top of everything, but would absolutely go out of her way to put you forward, compliment you, point you out in public situations whenever she felt it was valuable for the person. That was really unprecedented in my experience. Other people have a harder time sharing that space because it does feel like a competition. And some managers, men and women, feel that their quality or performance is really reflected by the people who work for them. I do think in these highly competitive times, everyone is much more anxious about their value and longevity. Just because you were great yesterday, it doesn't mean you're great today.

ROBERTA

As a Senior Vice President at a private bank, Roberta has worked in the financial services industry since the mid-1980's.

ROBERTA: After working in large corporate environments for many years, I jumped to a very small firm—there are only fourteen of us. While the change was initially daunting, I suspect the reason I'm enjoying this environment is because I worked in corporate America long enough and can understand why being part of a very small private group has a lot of benefits. But I don't know that I would fully appreciate the differences had I started my career in a small firm.

CONNIE: As you were going through the various places you worked, did you have a network of other women that helped you, guided you, or provided you any sort of support?

ROBERTA: Yes, I can think of several women who were great sounding boards. I still appreciate their counsel and their insights. There certainly is value in having female friends and support systems in the workplace. On the other hand, I have to say that I have mixed feelings about the notion of women having "dedicated" women mentors. This may be more effective in theory than practice. Effective mentor-mentee relationships are not arranged, they evolve.

CONNIE: Tell me a little more about that issue.

ROBERTA: First off, I'd like to think that the world has changed enough that men have come to appreciate having women at the table with them—we all think a little bit differently. And because we problem-solve a bit differently, we actually might come to a better solution at the end of the day. I have enjoyed working with many great male colleagues over the years. Frankly, work is more stimulating when you have both men and women at the table together.

CONNIE: Do you think that men trust women as much as they trust other men? Trust either a peer or someone else that they work with?

ROBERTA: I don't think that they distrust women or distrust their female colleagues, but it's different—the relationships are just different. I think that men can be less formal with one another than they can be with female peers in the workplace.

A New Paradigm for Ambitious Women

CONNIE: Do you think that women support each other as much as men support each other?

ROBERTA: No. Women do not necessarily have the equivalent internal networks within a corporation that senior male executives have. Women are also held to slightly different standards in terms of their corporate behavior. Women have to work harder to find suitable support networks. I did not experience senior women having the same kind of relations with female colleagues that men seem to have with their male peers.

CONNIE: Is there a place specifically for woman-to-woman networking?

ROBERTA: I think women are great networkers, and there are organizations that have evolved to connect women to women. The groups with which I am familiar focus on programs of interest to professional women. In fact, there may be more networking of this nature going on among women than men. Women have taken the initiative to move outside of their immediate workplace to engage with other women on a professional level.

LISA

Lisa's early careers included education, corporate communications, and corporate training. Since those earlier phases, she has shifted into executive roles of marketing, mergers, and acquisitions.

CONNIE: Tell me a little about how you got your confidence.

LISA: As a consultant, you get to sit shoulder-to-shoulder with the big boys right from the beginning, so I always was a partner. My confidence probably came from information. To some degree I was their partner without them having to fuss with me about other things. I was never at cross-purposes with them because I wanted the same things they wanted. That's also how I got paid—through their success. That success was my goal. So, my confidence came as a by-product of those relationships and experience.

CONNIE: What were some of the obstacles you faced that a male executive wouldn't have faced?

LISA: When I worked as an employee, the number-one frustration I experienced was being—the word I'll use is "uninformed." I felt the sidebar hall meetings and walk-by conversations between the men left me in the dark. Truthfully, I think a lot of it happened at the urinal! Yeah, that's where I could just imagine the conversation: "You know, we really ought to fly up and take a look at that other operation on Thursday." That could've been a passing comment made in some boy-to-boy way, but all too often I was only privy to the formal meetings. By the time we met, I felt out of the loop. I can count on one hand the meetings I attended where I *didn't* feel blindsided by *something*. The men's perspective was probably, "Oh, we thought we told you," "We thought you were there," or "Yeah, we talked about that; we were playing nine holes Friday afternoon and it just came up." I was either out of the loop or wasn't in the right place at the right time. One of my biggest obstacles was the continual catch-up game.

CONNIE: So you were disadvantaged for not knowing—even though they hadn't done anything to help you know?

LISA: It was always a jolt—that moment you realize you didn't know. I hated having to ask or admit to them or myself that I wasn't in the loop.

CONNIE: Is it accurate to say that the most insidious part is that they didn't even realize you weren't there?

LISA: Or worse, that they questioned whether I even need to be in the room at all. That's just how far I could take it. Politically it was never to my advantage to push this envelope—and say, "I think if you are going to have these conversations, and if you're going to reach some kind of decision, it should be done in a formal meeting."

CONNIE: Most women will relate to what you're saying—that communication is one of the more frustrating ways that women get shut out. In light of that, what would you advise women to do as a way of somehow getting this information? Is there a way that women can network among each other and then counteract being shut out?

LISA: I learned to play golf; I learned to play well. Gratefully, I was enough of an athlete that I could get out and not aggravate the situation by being slow or not understanding *all* the rules. I got to where I was with them as much as I could be, short of—as my term has now become—"at the urinal." I was as close as I could get to not missing those informal discussions. With the exception of one male who very much had a problem with women, I don't believe that exclusion was ever necessarily strategic on their part. I think the issue was that in these "informal" times, women are just not there. Did I get excluded from lunches? I did not. Did they shut the door if they knew I was within listening range? They did not. Did they purposefully say to each other, "Hey, go with me to the men's room while I run this new idea to run by you"? They did not. It was just that exclusion occurs if the structure of the company is not formalized enough. It is the "way of the world" and missing those times inhibits not just gaining information but wisdom and clarity about strategy. Women too often limit their breadth and scope of the world—business and industry—because they are so absorbed in the day-to-day job—they will miss lunch, miss network opportunities, and miss other real windows to stay in the game.

CONNIE: We all know that attire counts for something in the business world. What are your thoughts on this issue?

LISA: Somebody ought to come up with the *new* professional dress for women. While guys still look professional in a polo type shirt and khakis, women hear "business casual" and get lost! Today's professional females seem flailing for guidance in this flip-flop, tank-wearing, cutoff-wearing, cleavage-revealing world.

CONNIE: Can you comment on the career/family issues that women face?

LISA: That's the perfect double standard. Have we ever heard a man say, "I just don't know how I'll ever manage my career and family"? That would never fall out of a man's mouth. But if you talk about a woman being ambitious, that is seen as pretty ugly, frowned upon by men and women. There's something seen as a genetic disorder if a woman says, "I want that. I'm going after that.

I want to move up. I want to be the president." Career-inspired women struggle to find a mate that supports their aspirations and offers them a true partnership in their journey. I am very blessed to have a husband who, equally driven to succeed and accomplish, provides support and balance to my career.

CONNIE: The other half of the double standard is that if a woman isn't ambitious—if she has a more moderate level of ambition and wants a balanced life—people will say, "She isn't enough of a go-getter to put in a high position."

LISA: That's exactly right. And you know what? I've been guilty of it. I've been one of those leaders who will watch a woman who does not have my level of ambition or assertiveness or desire, and I have eliminated her as a viable candidate for promotions. And it doesn't have anything to do with family, because I had four women that worked for me that all had stay-home husbands. They had children and then were back at work. They were *the* breadwinners. My decision was based on the fact they were not career-minded. I've had to learn to respect that and support those women and be grateful for when and how they want to contribute. We need them as a part of the entire corporate body.

The other taboo I was going to mention was children. That's huge. I personally have one daughter, and I had outside help while raising her. I was very fortunate how it worked out, I didn't have a nanny, but I had women who came to the house and stayed with her. I traveled and left her with her grandmother. That was never going to be an issue for me. Another learning for me has to be to again appreciate that not all women are like me—some make the choice to minimize the corporate opportunities and focus on family.

CONNIE: Why is it that we women sometimes trust men more than we trust women?

LISA: I think it's because women are still playing by the girls' version of "the rules of the game," which are men's rules and men's norms and men's values. And as long as that culture exists, there will always be a dichotomy for women but not for men. Women still vie for the men's attention and appreciation and consider other women their competitors. These are old tapes and thinking, but it plays out every day in the workplace. It's as though women enter the corporate door and we turn into adolescent girls, clawing and biting to be most popular.

CONNIE: What about the benefits of leadership training?

LISA: I think the Center for Creative Leadership and the Harvard Business School have a framework that has merit and value and worth. It should combine financial thinking but still try to have that "draw" to meet all that is female. I'm not trying to get away from being female, but I am saying that as a working executive woman I would have preferred to have something that was going to help me think more strategically on the job.

CONNIE: Let's talk about trust and support. Is the moral of the story that women are especially vulnerable, and that if you take a stand precisely because you're a woman, there's probably no one who's going to take a bullet for you? Is that the big picture there?

LISA: I think that's very accurate. When the heat is on, no one moves away quicker than another woman. They *do* want to see the wreck of course, but they won't help you out of it. It is sad how few women will support other women at work. But it is the

A New Paradigm for Ambitious Women

men who will at least stand by and remark, "Girl, this is going to really hurt, but you know, you'll be ok. In fact I'll buy lunch next time, because you'll need it."

As I read over these interviews—and whenever I've read over the longer transcripts they're drawn from—I'm always tempted to "connect the dots" and find all the ways in which these six women's experiences are similar. And there are, in fact, some significant similarities present. I believe, however, that the differences among them are also important. These very accomplished women have different backgrounds, roles, duties, family/work challenges, aspirations, and other personal factors in play. There's no reason why what they face in the corporate world or how they intend to address the issues should align into exactly the same patterns.

Where does this situation leave us, then? I believe it leaves us with a fascinating, challenging, and promising conundrum.

In light of what I have learned over the last two years, what I learned during my 30 plus years in corporate America, and what I have learned from the personal stories of so many other women, it is truly amazing that so many women have managed to enter and be represented at nearly all levels of corporate America. We are only glaringly absent at the highest levels of leadership. Women have accomplished this in the face of business environments that were never designed with them in mind, and that in fact tend to isolate and then eliminate them from the executive levels. They have also survived and thrived in a broader culture that from the moment they are born begins to mold them into women who are primarily rewarded and recognized for being selfless and giving. What is not so well documented and understood is the strength and character that women possess in order to often be all things to all people . . .

and still find success and reward everywhere except the very top levels of our corporations. It takes a far stronger and determined and wise person to manage a truly balanced life. A life that gives the most and the best to both family and career at the right time and in the best manner possible. This is what is missing in the leadership of corporate America today. They are missing the wisdom, strength, and humility that women can bring to the table. The few companies that have truly learned to harness the power of men and women together understand the sustainable competitive advantage that they possess.

CONCLUSION

INDEPENDENCE DAY

Why haven't women found significant representation at the highest levels of corporations? This question is the core issue that prompted me to write this book, and it's the question we've circled around in each chapter as we examine some of the biological, cultural, and environmental factors that affect the numbers. I'll be the first person to say that there's no single, definitive answer. Maybe that's just the reality of any major social/political/interpersonal issue. At the same time, I'm 100% committed to "moving the needle" in ways that will foster the careers of individual women and, in addition, the careers of women as a group. I believe that as women have stronger representation in executive positions, those companies will become stronger in many ways.

In examining all the forces at work, I believe it's worthwhile for us to stand back for a moment and consider the history of our country. The United States of America has long been called "the land where dreams come true" and "the place where you can be anything you want to be." I believe that the promises embedded in these phrases remain bright with opportunity. At the same time, we women need to consider the remaining gaps between the promise and the reality. Consider this reference point: our country's Declaration of Independence. This document essentially created our nation, it's true—but it created not so much a nation "of the people, by the people, and for the people" (as Abraham Lincoln said less than 90 years after the Founding) but rather a nation "of the men, by the men, and for the men"—and then only if your skin happened to be white. Read the following sentence from the Declaration, and note the one word I've italicized:

> We hold these truths to be self-evident, that all *men* are created equal, that they are endowed by their Creator with certain unalienable Rights, that among these are Life, Liberty, and the pursuit of Happiness.

How ironic it is that the very creation of our country took place because the male colonials felt strongly enough about freedom to die for it—but then they denied so many other people, including women, the freedom that they themselves craved so intensely. How shortsighted—how blind, even—that the Founding Fathers encumbered women and non-white inhabitants of the new nation with burdens that these men sought to eliminate for themselves. How remarkable that the Declaration of Independence states outright that the oppressed have the right and the duty to "throw off such Government and to provide new Guards for their future Security"... yet those same men would have been astonished and probably outraged if their wives and sisters—the Founding Mothers by any other name—had demanded an equal share of rights at that time.

A New Paradigm for Ambitious Women

We know that women had their own place in the American colonies, and that place may well have given rise to some genuine sense of accomplishment and satisfaction among them. Such accomplishments and satisfactions, including those in the domestic sphere, have been part of women's lives since time immemorial. However, women's lives included severe restrictions as well. I have been reminded how severe life was for colonial and early-American women in the early days. As I review my family tree back to the 1600s, it becomes clear that the role of women was to provide offspring (read: members of the labor force) in large numbers. Many of my female ancestors had ten or more children . . . and then died at a relatively early age. In the aftermath of this country's founding, women gained rights and privileges only with the permission and approval (often grudgingly granted) of the men in power. (As Abigail Adams—an early champion of women's rights and, later, the wife of the second U.S. President, John Adams, wrote to her husband: "Remember the Ladies. . . . Do not put such unlimited power into the hands of the Husbands."

1848—The first Women's rights convention is held in New York[2]

1850—The Female Medical College of Pennsylvania is founded[2]

1910—Washington State grants women the right to vote[2]

1911—California grants women the right to vote[2]

1912—Kansas, Oregon, and Arizona grant women the right to vote[1]

1920—The 19th Amendment to the U.S. Constitution, granting women the right to vote nationwide, becomes law when it is ratified by two-thirds of the states.[1]

1963—The Equal Pay Act prohibits paying women less than men for the same job.[1]

1964—Title VII of the Civil Rights Act prohibits discrimination in employment on the basis of race or sex.[1]

1965—The Supreme Court's ruling (*Griswold v. Connecticut*) legalizes birth control for married couples in the United States.[1]

1972—Title IX of the Education Amendments bans sex discrimination in schools.[1]

1994—Congress passes the Violence Against Women Act, which fostered better investigation of crimes against women, increased pre-trial detention of the accused, imposed automatic and mandatory restitution on those convicted, and allowed civil redress in cases prosecutors chose to leave unprosecuted[2]

So far, so good ... but these were just a limited number of steps on the path, and such a long road to travel! And, as every woman knows, the journey is far from over.

One sign of the slow progress has been the fate of the Equal Rights Amendment, which states: "Equality of rights under the law shall not be denied or abridged by the United States or by any state on account of sex." The Equal Rights Amendment passed in the U.S. Senate and then in the House of Representatives; and, on March 22, 1972, the proposed 27th Amendment to the Constitution was sent to the states for ratification. But as for every other amendment since the 18th (with the exception of the 19th Amendment), Congress placed a seven-year deadline on the ratification process. The ERA received 22 of the necessary 38 state ratifications in the first year. But the pace slowed as opposition began to organize: the amendment gained only eight ratifications in 1973, three in 1974, one in 1975, and none in 1976. Following a three-year extension of the deadline (from 1979 to 1982), ratification failed. ["The History Behind the Equal Rights Amendment," http://www.equalrightsamendment.org/era.htm]

It's worth noting as well that even where women have equal *rights,* such as in having an equal right to legislative representation, we don't necessarily gain the desired outcome. In 2009, for instance, the 111th Congress included 17 women serving in the Senate and 73 women serving in the House of Representatives. This total of 90 seats equals only 17 percent of the 535 seats in Congress. These and other realities certainly prompt me—and many other women—to wonder how much has really changed in the 21st century.

Where does this situation leave us? I believe that an Independence Day for women is long overdue.

If I could take a magic wand and create this day for women, and if I could help foster the goal of finally achieving a world where men and women work side by side, and if reaching this goal allowed women's knowledge, skills, experience, and abilities to be *equally recognized* and *equally rewarded,* here's what I'd advocate:

PREPARE AND TRAIN

There's no alternative to first-rate education and training. You need to be both strategic in knowing your goals and earnest—even bullheaded—in accomplishing those goals. Make a game plan, acquire the skills you need, and establish your credentials as well. See this process as a long-term endeavor; you need to be a continual learner. If you want to be at the table, you need to understand the table stakes.

When I say "long-term endeavor," I'm not just referring to learning in a traditional, institutional sense. I also mean that you should attend leadership training programs designed for women only. These will give you insight, guidance, support, and recognition vital to your career. While it's true that some such leadership training programs can be for mixed groups, I believe nonetheless that women-only programs provide something critical that can't be obtained any other way. In women-only groups, you get to experience what being in the majority can do to help you gain power and influence. It's just like learning to swim: once you "get it," you will possess that skill forever. By contrast, it's very difficult to learn about power and influence when you are always in the minority.

In addition, you need to be open to informal training and learning of crucial sorts. Remember: information is powerful, and we all gain much of it through relationships, not through formal programs as such. The most spontaneous and casual conversations in your workplace may provide you with insights, data, context, and connections that will be indispensable to your success. The new world of social media should be a friend to women, but it may also make it easier for you to be left out. Pay attention to what goes on around you. Pay particular attention to your peers. Women are better at managing up and down than across. There is significant power and influence to be had with your peers, and these elements are very important. If you are successful, these people will become your subordinates one day, and you will need their allegiance. Likewise, one of these peers may some day become your boss. Look at them carefully. Whom do you need to cultivate? Start or participate in women's network groups. If your company doesn't have them, start one. There are many great companies that have such groups, and the women there will help you.

UNDERSTAND THE GAME

As we discussed earlier in this book, women sometimes feel that "playing the game" at work is tantamount to being manipulative. This attitude is a big mistake. It's true that some "players" can be manipulative as they "make their moves," but understanding the rules, moving strategically, building alliances, and understanding the "economy" present in any organization or culture isn't inherently wrong or even problematic. Indeed, it is completely inevitable—just part of what happens among people in any group. Men have clearer expectations about their role in the workplace because they understand that part of what happens is just "the game." They grasp that this is simply the nature of reality. It's important for women to do the same.

It's also true, however, that men expect women to see the workplace through their eyes. They expect women to play by "the guys' rules." And, to be frank, men expect to be in charge of the game. Why? Because that's how it's always been! In almost every human culture, boys are indulged during childhood and given precedence over girls in ways that foster a strong sense of entitlement as they grow up. Most organizations—whether in business, government, religious institutions, or anywhere else—have been set up by men to attend primarily to men's needs and to proceed according to men's agendas. Now that women are entering many of these institutions in larger and larger numbers, they are facing the men's rules. What, then, should you do? My strong recommendation: figure out the rules, learn to play them, and learn to win. As women, our culture has trained us to "give." We must learn to be "takers" as well. There's nothing wrong with that. It's just another skill to learn. And over time, we will change the model.

RECOGNIZE SOME UNCOMFORTABLE TRUTHS

Similarly, women need to understand that certain things may not be fair, but for the time being, they are still how things work. For instance, notions of equal opportunity are all well and good; unfortunately, equal opportunity doesn't necessarily result in equal representation and pay. If you expect the rules alone to guarantee full opportunities and inevitable benefits, you will wait . . . and wait . . . and wait . . . and wait . . . unless you take other actions on your behalf.

A related reality: diversity and inclusion are all well and good, too, and they have a place in helping all individuals work with each other. But they don't seem to impact executive representation of women. They may be necessary factors in supporting change, but they certainly aren't sufficient factors to cause change. Individual women—and women acting together as well—must go beyond diversity and inclusion to achieve real change.

Another uncomfortable truth is that your career ladder or path will be unique. As one women said: "It may be a journey with stops, starts, and turns." While there may be patterns to what women face over the course of their careers, each individual woman will need to shape her life to her own needs. Doing so will mean pushing up against expectations based on *men's* lifecycles and *men's* career paths. I believe as well that the variety of women's career paths is possibly greater now than it has ever been, and it's also greater than the variety of men's career paths. Coping with this reality means a willingness to engage in creative thinking of potentially radical sorts. It is both an opportunity and a challenge. An unwillingness to do so will probably leave you with limited options.

A New Paradigm for Ambitious Women

INSIST ON EQUALITY

Just "going with the flow" is no longer viable for most women, and it's certainly out of the question for ambitious women. You will need to push back against people who may try to limit you (regardless of whether their efforts are an expression of outright bias or something subtler, such as genuinely good intentions that still limit your options). For this reason, you should insist on equality in all parts of your life: in your work, in your marriage, and in your family. What you'll find when you take this approach is a new respect—from your spouse or partner, and from the people you work with and for. Learn to take what is yours. Be proud, be fearless, and lean on other women when you need to. Life has much to give, but it must be constantly and purposefully *pursued*.

You should also insist that your company—and, if possible, the wider business world—recognizes that women aren't adequately represented at executive levels. Insist on the setting of goals, responsibilities, accountabilities, and consequences.

In addition, you should insist that women support other women and women's organizations at every opportunity. It's all too common for women to see one another as rivals in the corporate world rather than as likely allies in fostering change. As many women have found when attending women-only leadership programs, we can be—and should be—willing, ready, and indeed eager to help one another, which ultimately will foster our careers.

CONNECT

As I noted elsewhere in this book, women are often so busy dotting all the i's and crossing all the t's in their day-to-day work that they forget how much of their success in the business world comes from connection with other people. What happens in the most informal and spontaneous settings often determines the individual's success or failure in the organization. For this reason, you should be alarmed when you are "left out of the loop." What doesn't happen is sometimes as important as what does happen. Do everything you can to remain part of the informal communication chain in your workplace. Begin your business networking and long-term relationship building immediately. This relationship building is one of the primary roles of business schools. It's also part of what you will gain from certain leadership programs. Since business relationships are about give-and take, be sure you take as much as you give. But above all else, put as much time and effort into building strategic, long-term, enduring relationships as you do any other facet of your work.

NOW!

If we were to adopt these approaches, would the result be an Independence Day for all women? I can't say for sure that such would be the result. I do believe that these actions would foster much more freedom for women in terms of both our work and our home lives. What I do feel strongly is that each woman can in some respects declare her own Independence Day and seek the freedom she wants and is entitled to.

The time for action is *now*. Our country has seen more cultural, political, and business molds broken in the last several years than over the last several decades. An opportunity lies before us. We only need to step into our power, recognize ourselves and our sisters, and declare independence in our homes, our families, and our organizations.

Are you ready?

ENDNOTES

1. "Milestones in U.S. Women's History," America.gov: http://www.america.gov/st/peopleplace-english/2009/February/20080325190828liameruoy0.3090631.html]) These rights and privileges have been hard won at every stage of American history. Here's just a brief glimpse of what has happened and how long the concessions have taken:

2. "Important Dates in Women's History" in http://www.pocanticohills.org/womenenc/dates.htm

APPENDIX 1

LEADERSHIP PROGRAMS for WOMEN

In Chapter 5, "Durable Relationships and Networks—and How to Build and Use Them," as well as elsewhere in this book, I've stressed the importance of networks for women in the corporate world. I've also described my views about leadership issues and how they impact women's careers. These are big, complex topics that I can't address in detail even in the course of a book. However, I'd like to mention three programs by name that I deeply respect and that I believe will make dramatic contributions to women's careers in the business sector.

SMITH COLLEGE WOMEN'S LEADERSHIP PROGRAMS

For almost thirty years, Smith College has provided executive leadership programs focused on women and their needs in the corporate world. Specific programs include The Smith-Tuck Global Leaders Program for Women, Women in Science, Technology and

Engineering; Leadership Consortium; and a variety of custom programs for individual companies. According to Iris Newalu, Director of Smith Executive Education, the Smith College programs are essentially a Women's Leadership Center. "Our programs focus on the challenges women leaders are actually facing as identified by the Fortune 500 companies we work with, our participants, and the best thought leaders in women's leadership today." Although the Smith programs "instill world-class strategic leadership, management, and technical competencies in its program graduates," according to Newalu, the female-only seminars and ancillary activities "afford women the chance to network with their real peers (other women leaders and high-potentials) from different companies, countries and industries in ways usually reserved only for their male counterparts."

WOMEN IN CABLE AND TELECOMMUNICATIONS (WICT)

Founded in 1979, WICT intends to advance the position and influence of women through proven leadership programs and services at both the national and local level. One component of the organization, the Betsy Magness Leadership Institute, is designed to elevate women leaders in the cable and telecommunications industry. Structured introspection, grappling with universal professional challenges, and the opportunity to shift perspectives within an empowering learning community enables Betsy Magness fellows to make the transition from effective managers to enduring leaders. The networks developed by the alumni of this Institute are among the strongest in the industry. WICT also administers an annual PAR Initiative that demonstrates the industry's commitment to **P**ay equity, **A**dvancement opportunities, and **R**esources for work-life support.

A New Paradigm for Ambitious Women

THE WOMEN OF TI FUND

Designed to foster women's advancement at even earlier stages than the Smith College and Betsy Magness programs. This organization focuses chiefly on closing the gender gap in science, technology, engineering, and math professions. The Fund's mission is to increase the number of girls graduating from high school who are entering a university-level technical degree program. Since the fund's inception, more than 300 girls have attended Advanced Placement (AP) physics camps, over 50 educators have participated in gender equity training, and more than 170 school counselors have attended engineering workshops. Future plans include packaging all three programs for implementation in additional school districts. The benefits of these programs have been remarkable. In the Dallas Independent School District (DISD), 57 girls took an AP physics exam in 2000 with a pass rate of only 12%,—30% below the boys. In 2007, following participation in the TI Fund's physics camp, 132 girls took an AP physics exam with a pass rate of 43%. Furthermore, girls who attended an AP physics camp and who also had teachers that utilized the gender equity practices passed the exam at the same rate as the boys. The pass rate of the boys who had teachers that utilized the gender equity practices also increased. The implications: the TI Fund's initiatives can have strong benefits for young women—and, intriguingly, for young men as well.

APPENDIX 2

FURTHER READING

Many business leaders and others have influenced my thinking about women's executive careers. Here is a selection of the books I have found most useful and interesting as I've explored the many interconnected topics that comprise this subject.

Ageenko, Ilieva I. *Connecting My Dots: A Woman's Leadership Guide for Multidimensional Success.* Bloomington, Indiana: Author House, 2009.

Barsh, Joanna and Susie Cranston. *How Remarkable Women Lead: The Breakthrough Model for Work and Life.* New York: Crown Business, 2009.

Barletta, Martha. *Marketing to Women, How to Understand, Reach, and Increase Your Share of the World's Largest Market Segment.* Chicago: Dearborn Trade Publishing, 2003.

Brisendine, Louann. *The Female Brain*, New York: Morgan Road Books, 2006.

———. *The Male Brain*. New York: Broadway Books, 2010.

Cronin, Lynn and Howard Fine. *Damned If She Does, Damned If She Doesn't: Rethinking the Rules of the Game That Keep Women from Succeeding in Business*. New York: Prometheus, 2010.

Dabbs, James M. "Salivary Testosterone Measurements in Behavioral Studies," in *Annals of the New York Academy of Sciences*, Vol. 694, September 1993.

Blanchard, Ken and Phil Hodges. *Servant Leader*. Nashville, Tenn.: Thomas Nelson, 2003.

Ehrenreich, Barbara. *Bait and Switch: The (Futile) Pursuit of the American Dream*. New York: Holt Paperbacks, 2006.

———. *Nickel and Dimed: On (Not) Getting By in America*. New York: Holt Paperbacks, 2008.

Fausto-Sterling, Ann. *Myths of Gender: Biological Theories about Women and Men* (Revised Edition). New York: Basic Books, 1992.

Fels, Anna. "Do Women Lack Ambition?" *Harvard Business Review*, April 2004.

Fiorina, Carly. *Tough Choices*. New York: Penguin Group, 2007.

Halpern, Diane F. *What Men Don't Tell Women About Business: Opening Up the Heavily Guarded Alpha Male Playbook*. New York: Wiley-Blackwell, 2008.

Hewlett, Sylvia Ann. *On Ramps and Off Ramps: Keeping Talented Women on the Road to Success.* Cambridge, Mass.: Harvard Business Press, 2007.

Ireland, Mardi S. *Reconceiving Women.* New York: The Guilford Press, 1993.

Lombardo, Michael M. and Robert W. Eichinger. *The Leadership Machine: Architecture to Develop Leaders for any Future.* Minneapolis, Minn.: Lominger Ltd Inc., 2000.

Moe, Karine and Dianna Shandy. *Glass Ceilings and 100-Hour Couples: What the Opt-Out Phenomenon Can Teach Us about Work and Family.* Athens, Georgia: University of Georgia Press, 2009.

Mooney, Nan. *I Can't Believe She Did That!: Why Women Betray Other Women at Work.* New York: St Martin's/Griffin, 2006.

Powell, Colin. *My American Journey.* New York: Ballentine Books, 2003.

Rako, Susan. *The Hormone of Desire: The Truth about Testosterone, Sexuality, and Menopause. New York: Three Rivers Press, 1999.*

Ruderman, Marian N. and Patricia J. Ohlott. *Standing at the Crossroads: Next Steps for High-Achieving Women.* San Francisco: Jossey-Bass, 2002.

Tarr-Whelan, Linda. *Women Lead the Way: Your Guide to Stepping Up to Leadership and Changing the World.* San Francisco: Berrett-Koehler Publishers, 2011.

Van Velsor, Ellen and Martha W. Hughes-James. *Gender Differences in the Development of Managers: How Women Managers Learn from Experience.* Greensboro, N.C.: Center for Creative Leadership, 1990.

ABOUT CONNIE WHARTON

Connie Wharton is one of the pioneer women who led the way into the highest levels of the corporate world. Beginning as a contract security guard for a Fortune 500 company, Ms. Wharton seized every opportunity to be successful in a male-dominated culture. She is now sharing her experiences, insights, and knowledge with other women. She is also asking the difficult questions of the corporate world about why there are still so few women in executive positions today.

Ms. Wharton has a unique background that included running a $500 million telecommunications business serving over 500,000 customers in 87 different municipalities. During her tenure with Time Warner Cable, she served as a Division President and ran one of the largest cable systems in the country. Prior to joining Time Warner Cable, Ms. Wharton served as Vice-President and General Manager for the Cox West Texas Region. During her eight-year tenure with Cox, she saw the West Texas organization triple in size. Before entering the telecommunications industry, Ms. Wharton spent twenty years with Texas Instruments, Inc. She progressed rapidly through the Human Resources ranks, and at the age of 37 she became the second woman in TI's history to be named

Vice-President. Additionally, she led TI's first diversity effort in the early 1990s. In a few short years, Texas Instruments won the nationally acclaimed Catalyst award.

Ms. Wharton has also been extremely active in civic and charitable organizations throughout her career. From serving on the advisory board of one of the largest private banks in Texas, to serving on the advisory board of the Rawls Business College at Texas Tech University, to being on the board of the nationally acclaimed Lubbock Reese Redevelopment Authority effort (the decommissioning and renovation of an Air Force base), her experience is broad and deep. She also served as the President of the Texas Cable Association.

Connie is a graduate of Southern Methodist University. She is also a graduate of the Women in Cable Telecommunications Betsy Magness Leadership Institute, as well as the Harvard Business School CTAM program. Connie and her husband Larry, an attorney, reside in Lubbock, Texas. They have two daughters.